Second Chances

ABRAMS IMAGE, NEW YORK

Also by Erin McHugh

One Good Deed
Like My Mother Always Said
Like My Father Always Said
Like My Teacher Always Said

Second Chances

**An inspiring collection
of do-overs that have made
people's lives brighter.**

ERIN McHUGH

Editor: David Cashion
Designer: Devin Grosz
Production Manager: Kathleen Gaffney

Library of Congress Control Number: 2017930326

ISBN: 978-1-4197-2413-8

Text copyright © 2017 Erin McHugh

Printed and bound in the United States
10 9 8 7 6 5 4 3 2 1

Abrams books are available at special discounts when purchased in quantity for premiums and promotions as well as fundraising or educational use. Special editions can also be created to specification. For details, contact specialsales@abramsbooks.com or the address below.

ABRAMS The Art of Books
115 West 18th Street, New York, NY 10011
abramsbooks.com

To every one of us who ever said,
"Let me try again, just one more time."

Introduction

It can be anything, a second chance. It starts when you're a kid, hoping for do-overs like one more swing at the ball, another tryout for the play, making up with your best friend after a squabble—things you think are going to change your life. That's how important another go at it feels. And at the time, it was.

When we look back, these breaks seem simple, so inconsequential. As adults, though, we often tend to think of second chances as opportunities on a grander scale: to right a failure, roll the seemingly Sisyphean rock back up the hill, or—fingers crossed—get back that thing or person we let slip away. But second chances can be so much more than that.

First and foremost, they are about learning and realizations. A second chance can be eye-opening and glorious, about recoveries of all kinds, a one-time chance to see things a different way. And another go-around doesn't always have to mean looking for the same result, either.

Second Chances is meant to inspire its readers—and hopefully help them strive for something new, better, bigger. Help to see the positive, appreciate the unexpected, perhaps feel gratitude where one thought there was nothing to be grateful for. Within these pages, you'll find people who have found new glimmers of light after losing their homes in fires, or suffering through Hurricane Sandy. The realizations that their families are safe and that they have new bonds with their communities opens up a new part of these people's souls. And there are also contributors who have found that they have to do very little, really, to right a wrong or implement an improvement that will give them peace or a new outlook. I urge you to open your mind up to what a new beginning is—not always so linear as "step one, step two." Start to realize that every bend in the road is part of what comes next.

But not every second chance needs to be so momentous and life-changing. Some folks here have said they try to be aware of new and more modest options daily. And you will find lightheartedness in these pages, believe me. You'll read stories that will delight you and many others that will feel very familiar. Perhaps familiar enough to make you reassess and try again.

Each one of these contributions is the story or musing of an ordinary person—some who have been through some very extraordinary things, and others, well, they've got plans to change things around in life. The unifying thread is that they all have an ending that allows the storyteller to go forward with his or her life. Occasionally, it's not what we'd normally call a Happy Ending, but as one person noted about her experience, "The sun came up again the next day, and then the next day, and the next day." And sometimes that is enough to begin a path to greater fulfillment.

And I can tell you that people found very different ways to

tell their stories. Some were eager to recount well-worn tales they found comfort in. Others needed encouragement, then wrote to me later and said that having put words to paper about their experiences for the first time ever was cathartic in a way they never expected. And still others I had lengthy dialogues with, gently prodding them to recall and finally spill out their experiences. Several storytellers needed help writing about themselves, so we composed drafts together and they expanded and edited until their contributions felt like the stories they knew so well. I think I can say it has been an extremely heartfelt experience for all of us.

Of course, part of the purpose of this book is my desire—for myself and others—to not have to look back later and say, "I wish I had . . ." After writing her story, one woman said to me: "Every moment offers a second chance; no feeling is final. We are on a journey to make ourselves more conscious, so every moment holds the potential for a new way."

If I were to say one thing about second chances, it would be this reminder: Everybody's had one—and everybody's got plenty more.

ERIN McHUGH
New York City, Spring 2016

Second Chances

The Dawn of a New Day

I believe that I am given a second chance every day.

Every morning, I wake up and think that I can do it better today, do it right, whether it's my job or the people I touch, or don't touch—or maybe it's exercise, or what I eat or drink, a kindness, a new interest, or how I relate to my children, or something I learn about myself.

Each day is a new beginning. Trite? Maybe.

But it works for me.

—ELLEN

Wild Child Redux

Once upon a time in the snowy mountains of the north lived a wild child who loved to ski. One cold and rainy January day, she decided to hit the slopes. She got a little ahead of herself on what would be her only run that day, hit some ice going way too fast, and fell hard, ending up in the trees—lucky to have not actually hit one—with a severely broken leg. She was rushed to the hospital, where she would remain for the next ten days post–emergency surgery.

One metal plate and nineteen screws later, she was out of the hospital and on crutches. This state of being would last about a year, which was followed by another surgery to implant yet another plate. Finally, after two years of healing, all the hardware was removed from her leg and the real recovery began. Her doctors cleared her for physical activity, and because she hadn't been very mobile for two years, she felt as though she had been given another chance, and she was itching to get her legs moving again. So she started slow and learned how to walk again, then how to run again. Once her atrophied muscles bulked up and her range of motion returned, she signed her sorry ass up for the New York City Marathon.

She dedicated all of her free time to training and was determined to run that damn race, and she did, finishing in four hours and sixteen minutes. It was one of the most special days of her life. The weather couldn't have been better and the crowd couldn't have been more cheerful. Friends and family were there to cheer her on along with perfect strangers. And though she crossed the finish line, she hasn't stopped running. Of course, that wild child is me.

—MARTHA

I Dreamed of Africa

I suffer from chronic wanderlust that has taken me all over the world. My hardworking career as a real estate agent in the Hamptons allowed me the freedom to travel as long as my checkbook was topped up. I always had photos of the next destination posted on my desk at work and hoped that, if I used the phone successfully, the deals would get done and it would be wheels up for me!

Time moved so quickly, and all of a sudden I turned forty years old. I was successful and enjoyed my freedom as a single woman who was not tied down to a family. I was perfectly happy moving about my life . . . until I wasn't but didn't know it. Selling large second homes to very rich people who had every comfort was no longer a challenge or exciting. It was time for a life change, but I couldn't figure out what change I wanted or needed.

So I booked another trip. I had traveled on many horseback-riding safaris, but Africa was my favorite. The frequent chaos and poverty is balanced by the beauty and richness of the tribal cultures, wild animals, and generous people.

Determined to find my purpose, I researched volunteer projects all over the world. A project in Namibia run by Elephant Human Relations Aid was flexible enough that we also did work at the local school. It was a government-run boarding school (in rural communities in Africa, most schools are boarding schools since students live too far away to walk to school) that was not well funded and had very scant resources. From the minute I met the students, I knew something in my life was about to change.

I am a strong proponent of women in power and as leaders. I felt I needed to help the girls at the A. Gariseb Primary School put their future in front of them and dream big. Just because they were in the middle of the desert with little exposure or a promising future in the bigger world didn't mean they shouldn't try to achieve it—in fact, just the opposite!

At the school, I was a magnet for these girls and their smiling, promising faces. I loved when they all rushed up to me with little Valentine notes on tiny postage stamp–size scraps of paper. They always had a lovely flair: "Plis kip me in your hart fo eva." They always had butterflies, flowers, hearts, and, usually, uncanny drawings of me with them and "frends fo eva." They never asked for anything. Just a simple declaration that we were friends and that I would not forget them.

In my "back home" life, I was also on the board of our local library, and at that time, we were about to build a new addition. While sitting in a decrepit old cement school building on a three-legged chair propped up by a pail as its fourth leg, I kept thinking that these children were in need of a simple library with books that would expand their knowledge. "Learn to read, read and grow, grow and learn" became my mantra and theirs, too. So I set about sending books to Africa with a small amount of donated books from my library friends. It filled a room at the school we had painted in bright colors. On the wall, we painted, "Learn to read, read and grow, grow and learn."

These girls would run up to me in the schoolyard with their tattered books and blurt out passages at top volume for all the world to hear—proudly showing they had mastered not only reading but amazing self-confidence and poise.

We continued our aid to the school, and after ten years, we had renovated the dormitories, replumbed the showers and lavatories, and built a computer room, a playground, and more.

But my proudest moment happened when I was walking down a street and heard two girls calling my name. Most of the girls in the first group had either ended their primary school careers and returned to their farms or headed to high school—"Big School," they called it. These two girls were tall and skinny and in their "Big School" uniforms, standing proud and ready to take on the world. They reminded me who they were and what it meant for them to learn and read at that library with those books. It worked: They were dreaming big—and I knew they would succeed. My second chance was their first in having someone believe in them. It made me believe in myself as well.

—DOREEN

They never asked for anything. Just a simple declaration that we were friends and that I would not forget them.

The Fifty Year Reunion

1961–1965: Catholic high school

The nuns arranged classrooms alphabetically, so I, Nancy B., sat in front of Charlie B. for four years. We became fast friends, all because of the alphabet.

Charlie was outgoing and very, very funny. I was shy, quiet, and had to be well-behaved because my mother worked at the school; the nuns brought every move I made to "the good woman" in the business office.

Charlie and I began to exchange letters after high school—which led to dating when Charlie came home from college during the summers. He has said since that the first piece of jewelry he ever bought "for a lady" was for me. It was a gold necklace with one pearl. He mailed it . . . but I never received it.

I went to nursing school, and during my senior year there, I became engaged to the boy I had dated in high school. Charlie came back home and heard that I was getting married and was sad, but then he left to join the navy. I married in 1969 and had three children. Charlie relocated to California, met his wife, and had three children of his own.

Neither marriage worked out as well as we had hoped. Over the years, Charlie and I corresponded—prompted by parents passing away and, later, when I chaired a high school fundraising event. I'd always promised to attend the high school reunions . . . but never did. I think we both sometimes wondered what life might have been like if we'd married each other.

Charlie left me a message on our class's fiftieth reunion Facebook page: He was planning on attending and wondered if I'd like to get together for lunch with him and a third classmate. He still didn't know that I was divorced. Prior to that visit, Charlie called and we talked for two and a half hours. When we met for lunch, it was like nothing had changed in fifty years. Every day since, he has texted me in the morning and called each evening—and we have made several trips cross-country to visit. We are still best friends—with a little something else—and the romance continues.

Oh, and last Christmas? I received a gold necklace with one pearl. Finally.

—NANCY

Coming Home

This is a story for all those who think you can't go home again.

After college, I decided to do what millions of eager twentysomethings have done seemingly forever: I moved to New York. I loved it, and for a long time, it loved me back. I became a publicist, and I reveled in it. Every booking, feature, interview I got felt like a small victory. But, after years of riding the subway, sky-high rents, and exhausting dating rituals, I began to feel like the stresses of city life outweighed those victories—outweighed even those few magical moments, like when you're leaving a glittering party with your best friend, looking fabulous and buzzed on champagne. I moved farther away, to Windsor Terrace in Brooklyn, looking for suburban quiet and cheaper rents while I figured things out. I found myself making the trek to the great new restaurants and parties less and less. And I didn't miss them. By now, I had realized that I really wanted to work for myself, and work in a more creative capacity (even the exciting world of PR can become a little rote). I had made a lot of connections at my job, and I decided to start my own business. I got several clients right away, but it became clear that the jobs that I wanted were never the ones that paid the most. I didn't want to end up in another rut (or in debt!), so something else in the equation had to change.

I didn't really plan to move back home to Baltimore; if you had asked me five years before, I probably would have said it would never happen, that New York was the endgame for me. But now I had my life a little more in gear, and I found I could take my business anywhere. I found that I missed my family, especially my brother. Then my grandfather got sick, and when he passed away and I saw what it did to my father, it convinced me further that I wanted to be nearer to those I loved.

But that was just part of it. I began to really *see* Baltimore. I live a block from Patterson Park, an Audubon sanctuary, and I hear the birdsong every morning from my sunny home office on the second floor of my row house. I'm also a block away from my favorite pizza place in the city, and a five-minute after-dinner walk away from the Canton waterfront promenade. Baltimore's food, art, and start-up scene is exploding, which is perfect for my own fledgling business. Formerly very industrial, Baltimore is now home to major companies and has a thriving tech, design, and literary community. I suddenly realized that moving to my birth city was more than a convenient solution. I saw that I could really contribute, make an impact, and have a chance to help make it a better place for all residents. So I'm home in Baltimore, making a life of my own design, and every day feels filled with possibility.

—MARISA

The Old Hotel

In the mid-1970s, I found myself working for a lifelong friend making—of all things—candy sculptures, and as an offshoot, candy-house kits. Go ahead and laugh, but by the time this business started, she had already been featured in *People* magazine for building a seven-foot candy George Washington; a life-size castle in Macy's Santaland in Herald Square; and every Christmas, we worker bees would go and toil in Bloomingdale's windows, constructing house after gooey house. It was nutty—and a blast. Then things got serious.

The family of my candy-business friend owned a large and rambling old hotel, and they bought a beautiful Tudor manor house nearby, putting their daughter in charge of its rebirth as a second hotel. I was invited along for the sometimes bumpy but always interesting ride. Back then, it was an imposing old place, open only in the summer. Its guests were often there to enjoy the famed local music and dance festivals—or often they were the famous people actually appearing at those venues. I had previously worked as a cook at a small inn, so I was assigned to be the chef de cuisine. We served only breakfast, afternoon tea, and totally over-the-top multicourse picnics to take to the concerts. Still, I would get calls down in the kitchen from the guests. "We know you don't serve dinner, but it's our twenty-fifth anniversary, and

we would love it if you could just make us a chateaubriand."
We were in the LUXURY service industry now, trying to make
something of this hotel, so the customer was always right, and
the answer was ALWAYS yes. "Of course," I'd say cheerily, and
I'd hop in my VW Beatle to run to the market and gather what
was needed to whip up a three-course extravaganza.

The whole venture had a seat-of-the-pants feeling, but my
friend had vision, know-how, and a lot of stick-to-it-iveness.
We were young, and it was fun. She kept at it, but I eventually
left, went back to my hometown, got married, and had children, and though she and I remained very close, I moved on
to different jobs in a different life.

Years went by—in fact, decades went by!—and occasionally, I'd get a call from Ann, my old friend and boss, to come
back and work at the hotel. I'd tell her thanks, but I loved
my job—then the calls began to come closer together. So
one day more than thirty years later, Ann was on the phone
once again. This time, my job was about to end, the kids were
grown, and I needed a change. Still, it sounded so crazy to
me. "Ann," I said, "what would this job even be?" She paused
a minute, and then said, "Oh, Mimi. Sometimes I don't even
know if the *lampshades* are ripped!"

For some reason, I understood that—she was just over-
whelmed. And so I packed up and returned to join Ann once
again. I became part of the management team of a hotel that
is now world-renowned, has more stars and awards than you
could count, boasts one of the top wine cellars in the country, is open year-round, of course, and has become one of the

go-to hotel destinations in the country.

Obviously, the experience has been decidedly different this time around, but Ann has crafted a jewel, and to join her and be given another chance to make it perfect has been a very unexpected joy. From candy houses to five-star hotels— who would have guessed?

—MIMI

Growing Young

Because my now-grown children had been spending so much time at the dojo learning the martial art judo, I decided to jump in, too, and it turned out I earned an orange belt at the age of fifty. To top it off, it was presented to me by a former Olympian! I felt accomplished as well as youthful and strong. Plus, I got to spend more time with my kids.

—DENISE

Never Too Late

Someone once said, "It is never too late for anything."

Fortunately, those words came back to me when, at the age of thirty-one, upon the death of my husband, I found myself totally responsible for raising four children alone. Of course, we all were devastated, and I had to figure out how best to carry on. Having only secretarial training, I knew I needed the college education I had rejected years earlier. Although I probably could have gotten a job as a secretary, that would have meant being away from the children twelve months a year with only vacation time together. I thought that if I were able to become a teacher, I could be with them entire summers and school vacations.

Being married to a civil engineer made me realize how important further education is, and made me consider following up on the idea of becoming a teacher. At the time, it seemed an impossible challenge. Since there weren't too many choices available, I decided to try the impossible. But I had so many doubts: Would I be admitted as a college student at all? Could I handle the course work? Could I schedule classes while my children were in school? So I started with just one evening class—and I passed. Then two more classes the next semester—again I passed. And finally, after finding a good babysitter, I became a full-time student.

My children were cooperative with housework, we gave up many social events, and together we lived a jam-packed but happy life. To my surprise, with many hitches and glitches, I received a bachelor's degree that enabled me to teach English at a high school for thirteen years and then at a community college for another sixteen years. With help from my children and extended family, I was given a great opportunity and a second chance in life.

—DIANE

Sweet Revenge

Most second chances are redemptive. They allow a repeat in order to attain a deeply sought goal or repair a fault.

I have had many of these small good fortunes in my life. Almost daily, I have the need to double back and get it right, and I am grateful for those opportunities when I recognize them.

Another kind of second chance, however, is an opportunity for revenge. These are mostly best put aside, but in one instance in my life, the chance for revenge left me with some satisfaction and the feeling of getting even. I don't regret it much. Perhaps I should.

I had just turned sixteen, and I was flipping burgers at the neighborhood fast-food franchise of a national chain. Punching in and out, uniforms, a paycheck, and getting to hang with my buddies was new and all fairly exciting. We were having a good time and taking very little of it seriously.

My friend and coworker Elaine had just turned seventeen, and we rustled up a cake and a few candles and crammed into the small break room and sang the song. It all felt swell watching Elaine enjoy the spotlight. As we were set upon by the manager on duty, Melvin, we scrambled to get back to our workstations. Mel was a letch, an older married man who would leer at any of the high school girls I worked with and make everyone feel like they needed a shower. Mel asked

Elaine how old she was and made a very forward remark and a rude invitation for when she turned eighteen. I jumped in between him and her and called him many unflattering names. He was much bigger than me, and not impressed, and I'm sure his anger was about to run over. I escaped a slug but was fired on the spot and told to never return. Expelled from the club. Jobless.

I drove across town to the other burger joint, and in a few days, I was manning a grill again. I was back to filling my pockets with the minimum wage, but I was plotting revenge. The Christmas holidays were a few short weeks away, and I bided my time and hatched a plan. I needed a second chance.

When it got closer to the busy holiday season, I asked my current boss if I could take a few days off. With some schedule swaps with coworkers, I managed several free days. I returned to my former burger joint, begged Mel for my job back, and told him I'd reformed. Mel even admitted a fault or two. He gave me that second chance and let me start the next day. I signed up for a full load of work shifts. When Saturday came around, the busiest day, I clocked into work all decked out in my uniform. I waited until the height of the lunch rush. At the busiest moment, I loaded up every inch of space on all four grills with every piece of beef I could find and slipped out the back door to the parking lot. As I drove away, I beeped my car horn at Mel, who of course had a quizzical look on his face as he watched from the door. It wasn't a noble Norma Rae moment, but it sure felt good, and from the stories my friends told me later, it gave them some stolen smiles watching Mel scramble to man the grill for the rest of the day. He didn't last long after that. Mel's kind of sexual harassment isn't tolerated in the workplace much today, thankfully.

Many years later, at a speaking engagement, a man about my age came up to me and said, "Thank you." He explained that he was Elaine's brother and said that he remembered me from the incident on Elaine's seventeenth birthday. He remembered how much she needed that job. He remembered how relieved she was to be left alone at work after that.

—JOE

Most second chances are redemptive. Almost daily, I have the need
to double back and get it right,
and I am grateful for these opportunities when I recognize them.

Making the Grade

When I was a sophomore in college, I applied to a fiction writing seminar with one of the tenured figureheads of the English department. K. was a sublime image of Ivory Tower professorship, all arched eyebrows, vaulted forehead, and imperious wit; he who sat on the porch of the now-razed literary review office each morning, puffing an enormous cigar, and who had written multiple novels and articles adapted into successful Hollywood movies. We rapt observers of K. speculated endlessly about his swashbuckling authorial exploits as we drank cheap malt liquor and shivered in our dorm rooms through the sunless Ohio winter.

I was one of twelve sophomores accepted, and the only dour philosophy student amid perky English majors. We met once weekly for three hours, and we were all still getting acquainted when we began our third assignment. K. had been extremely clear that we were under no circumstances to miss class or fail to turn in exercises; each session missed and each missed assignment would lead to the irreparable loss of half a letter grade.

Despite that threat echoing menacingly in the distance, I remained a college sophomore with full foolishness intact, and when the time came for the third session, I had but one unfinished and very undistinguished exercise. Riddled with anxiety, I made what passed for a decision: Better to skip the class than turn in such a disappointment.

K. was an old-schooler who gave out notes handwritten in smudgy pencil, so I figured that he was unlikely to check e-mails, and I could thusly get away with not sending him one explaining myself. I tiptoed around campus for the next week in fear of being spotted from his smoky porch, and ultimately finished the draft. My plan: Arrive fifteen minutes ahead of the next session to talk to K. This strategy had paid prior dividends; most of the college's professors were of a more genial sort, and I believed that it would continue to work.

I arrived at his office as planned before the next class. I entered, and as he turned, I saw him darken. "Where the hell were you last week?" he growled. I began to recite my litany of excuses, but, "That's all bullshit," K. spat back, "and this is completely unacceptable." Without exception, he loudly derided each of my academic failures in turn. Finally, apparently spent, he looked at me and delivered the coup de grâce: "This is the most insulting thing anyone has ever done to me." With that, he snatched my draft out of my hands and unceremoniously booted me out.

I sat in class, alternating between horror and an insane variant of pride that I, of hundreds of pupils over the past twenty-odd years, had managed to wound the great and terrible K. so singularly with my foolishness. I considered that he had exaggerated his closing statement, but insincere people cannot quite manage that facial shade of eggplant.

I resolved not to allow my distinction as Most Insulting

Individual of All Time stand as my tombstone, and to his credit, K. gave me opportunities to get back into good graces (following a two-week period of total frost). I monastically attended class, edited my classmates' work, and finished my assignments, eventually turning in a linguistically confusing short story about a group of fishermen marooned on their trawler in a storm and forced to confront their land-based addictions and infidelities as they awaited rescue. Though the result was lacking revelation or cohesion, K. apparently liked it enough that he began to address me, almost warmly, as "Buddy," rather than barking my last name at me.

Final grades eventually arrived; he was true to his word. For my sins, I received a B+, but in his moment of earlier disappointed rage, K. had forced me out of my complacency, and for that, I have nothing but gratitude.

—SIMON

He had forced me out of complacency, and for that, I have nothing but gratitude.

The Double Rescue

What happens when two second chances meet?

A puppy named Iggy was born in a Dallas, Texas, shelter that was overrun before the ice storm of 2013 hit. He had three siblings, and the four of them were part of the largest flight of dogs to ever land at John F. Kennedy International Airport. It was all over the news in Dallas and New York. I didn't see it on TV, but my heart felt him coming.

I had been thinking of getting another dog, and by "another," I mean the first one in more than twenty years. I gave my last dog up to a family with a farm when apartment living and a new baby rocked Bonnie Blue's world so much, she acted up like some spaniels will and snapped at my newly crawling son. Being a (mostly) single working mom, I never felt like I could do justice to a pet dog.

So, on the morning of Christmas Eve 2013, I woke up and checked my e-mail. There was a message from ARF, our local rescue shelter, with a list of all the new dogs up for adoption that day. This one dog, Atom, had a blurry picture—he was too wiggly to pose—and at only eight weeks old, weighed just five pounds. I deleted the e-mail.

Two hours later, I stood in my son's bedroom doorway.

"Um," I said, and he looked up from his game. "I think I found my dog."

We went off to ARF, which opened just as we got there, and asked to see the litter. They were all so cute, but I knew Atom (his pre-Iggy birth name) right away. As soon as I held him, he was mine; we both knew it. His happy face and bright brown eyes and round little belly were adorable, of course, but there was something else. We were a team from the moment we met.

—KIM

Nancy Takes a Hike

When you find yourself in your sixties, time takes on new meaning. It is stunningly clear that life doesn't go on forever. At sixty, you are midway between forty and eighty. Bones begin to creak, blood pressure and other things rise. Strange, unmentionable things are happening to the temple that is your body. You realize that time is finite and you can't keep putting things off.

Shortly after I turned sixty, I realized that I wanted to mark my sixty-fifth birthday in December 2011 with an epic act that would combine physical activity with reflection on how to use the next twenty years, should I be lucky enough to experience them in good health. Walking across the United States fit the bill perfectly.

I shared the idea with my son, Casey, who thought it was cool. Then, one night in February 2010, at dinner with candles lit and the fireplace flickering, I put the idea out to my husband, Lincoln. Lo and behold, he was unbelievably receptive, and over many dinners, we had fun exploring the practicalities of how we'd do it.

Choosing Route 20 was easy. It passes within a couple miles of our house. It's a cross-country route that's full of history. From Boston to the Pacific coast of Oregon, it traces the westward embrace of this continent by the people and ideas (good and bad with the benefit of hindsight) that created our country.

So, one cold morning in February 2011, I stepped out from the waterfront in Boston and walked 7.5 miles to Watertown. Walking just a few days here and there, it took me until the following April to make it past Albany.

Fast forward, it's 2016. I turn seventy this year, and I'm about to cross the Snake River from Idaho to Oregon. Nearly 3,000 miles of Route 20 lie behind me. Although I've occasionally deviated from that road, it took me across the Mississippi, 425 miles through Nebraska, and will be my guide through vast, empty eastern Oregon. One day this year, it is very likely that Lincoln and I will splash into the Pacific in Newport, Oregon . . . one mile west of the official end of the road.

While I've been on this journey, things have happened. My mother died, my father died, my younger sister died, one of my businesses grew, another sputtered, and my son got engaged.

Each year that I've stepped back onto Route 20, it's a fresh moment to experience muscle soreness, blisters, relearn how to pack my daypack, and coexist with Lincoln in the used RV (named Moby) we bought in western Iowa. Every day, I'm out exploring America one step at a time. I'm not sure I've discovered the secret to living the perfect life in my aging years, but a few hundred miles still stretch ahead . . . and each one of them is another chance for an epiphany.

—NANCY

My Chameleon Life

My charming biological father was a psychopath who possessed a vicious and violent temper. He was motivated without provocation to beat me and my sister, who bore the brunt of his anger from her attempts to defend us. His footsteps toward our room sounded an unsettling alarm for me to retreat to the closet or under the bed.

As a child, I was short, fat, and wore glasses and thick-soled orthopedic shoes. I was always the last person standing when sides were chosen for relay races. Evidently, my father considered me an imperfect child, and so he deprived me of the food that my slender brother and sister freely enjoyed. This deprivation caused me to become bulimic in my twenties, a condition I fortunately overcame.

Somehow, my mother found the strength to rid us of his ever-present threat. With a restraining order in place, the authorities aggressively escorted my father from the house, and we went into hiding. A dear friend finally took us in. I was ten. My mother eventually enrolled me at a private all-girls Catholic high school. Again, I was an outcast, so I immersed myself in the study of art and photography.

I did not finish college, but decided that, against all odds, I was going to be a television news photographer. Breaking into what had been a male-dominated industry in the late

1970s was a feat unto itself, but a CBS affiliate had confidence in my ability and gave me my start. Then, in 1983, a national network beckoned. NBC hired me and moved me to Dallas/Ft. Worth, where I was alone—very alone. Most of my colleagues were either married or dating someone, and like so many lonely people, I sought companionship in a bar. No amount of alcohol could fill the void in my heart.

I was so incredibly needy during that time. I became a chameleon, transforming into whatever type of person I thought a man wanted so he would love me.

And then I finally met my future husband. He was unlike any man I had ever met. He was a successful businessman, kind, considerate, generous, and possessed an infectious laugh. He helped me find my smile again. We had a big Texas-style wedding and settled into a very upscale area where the social scene centered around golf, parties, and drinking to excess. I drove a Mercedes, lunched at the country club, and was president of the garden club.

I took over and grew my husband's company, but working together produced constant conflict. My husband's home winemaking hobby suddenly turned professional, and before I knew it, he was plowing up the "north forty" and planting a vineyard. I wrote a business plan, we built a tasting room, and when our first harvest came in, we opened a winery. I now drank for a living. But our life was tainted . . . tainted with bitterness, resentment, and anger. I had given up my career and left my home and my friends in Dallas to move and to marry the man who I thought was the man of my dreams. Eleven years later, I found myself alone again, without a husband, a job, or a home. I got a fund-raising job with, appropriately, an organization that served abused children.

My first darkest day of this period was when I was arrested for public intoxication in the middle of town at four o'clock in the afternoon. I spent the worst night of my life in the county jail. I had many rehab experiences over the coming years, and I eventually lost literally everything.

And then an old friend was prompted to look for me after years of being out of touch—and found me because my last DUI showed up on a Google search. She brought me to Florida to a shelter for victims of domestic violence and chemical dependency. Upon leaving the facility, I was still unable to stop drinking. My friend continued to help and guided me to a Christian program called Celebrate Recovery. It was there that I found love, understanding, and hope.

I just celebrated six years sober. While I still experience anxiety, depression, and other aftereffects from the abuse, which has prevented me from seeking gainful employment, I am *not* drinking.

We are slaves to the past by our own choosing—and I have drawn a line in the sand and now say, "That is who I was, and this is who I am now." My past does not define me, and through it, like sand shapes a pearl, I have been raised up and restored.

—PATTIE

We are slaves to the past
by our own choosing.

A Tale of Gratitude

Anthropologist Margaret Mead once said that a relationsip between sisters is "probably the most competitive relationship within the family, but once the sisters are grown, it becomes the strongest relationship." My older sister, Nancy, and I seemed stuck on the "competitive" part. Now we both needed to change that. By some odd confluence of the universe, my new focus on gratitude coincided with Nancy discovering mindfulness. My ambitious and successful businesswoman sister had started meditating every night and taking yoga classes. She even had a new consulting company focused on mindful leadership. Since both of us were trying to see the world through a more positive lens, we wondered if that filter could change our relationship with each other. We talked about trying to become the kind of sisters who talked and shared and cared.

So on an early December Friday, I took an Amtrak train to Washington, DC, for a "sisters weekend"—a phrase that, for me, hit about an eight on the Richter scale. Hang out together just for fun? The last time I remembered doing that, she was nine years old and I was five. A lot of water passed under many bridges since then, and we had our resentments and piques. We could each make a list of what the other had done wrong. But focusing on our past problems led nowhere, and we had nothing to lose by trying to be positive and appreciate each other. The gain might be much-wanted sisterly support.

For Nancy and me, that became the message of the weekend—appreciating the good in the moment rather than fussing about the past.

At one point, Nancy brought up an incident between us that had bothered her from years past. I had no defense—it was from long ago. Siblings typically let resentment linger, reliving when the other person let us down, ignored a need, said the wrong thing. But instead of recalling incidents gone wrong, I thought we needed memories gone right. I suggested we could restore our relationship by focusing on the times together that we felt grateful.

"Here's my gratitude memory of you," I said. I recounted a childhood night long ago when our grandpa had just died. Scared and sad, I couldn't get to sleep, and Nancy took out her music box, one of her most cherished possessions, and let me play the tinkly tune.

"You'd never let me play with your music box before," I told her.

"You were so little, you would have broken it."

"But you let me that night, because you knew it would cheer me up. I was too young then to say thank you, so let me say it now."

Nancy nodded, getting the point.

"How about you? I guess if you have no grateful memory, we might as well give up," I said.

But Nancy recalled a time when her three children were

very young, and she was in a tough situation, and I flew down from New York to see how I could help.

"I really appreciated that. So many other things got in the way afterward, but I knew that day you really cared," she said.

I put my arm around my sister and gave her a hug. Holding on to memories like the night of the music box or the day of the flying down gave us something to appreciate again. With that as the new basis for sisterhood, we could move forward.

We'd wasted a lot of time over the years annoyed by each other's mistakes and failings. But how much better to appreciate the moments of kindness and warmth—and hold on to those.

—JANICE KAPLAN from *The Gratitude Diaries*

Instead of recalling incidents gone wrong, I thought we needed memories gone right. I suggested we could restore our relationship by focusing on the times together that we felt grateful.

Waiting It Out

In 2003, I was working as a part-time magazine editor and hoping for a big break in publishing. One summer day, a colleague alerted me to a job announcement on Brass Ring: Books Editor at AOL. Amazing! A job in books that was right down the road from my Northern Virginia home instead of in Manhattan. I dusted off my résumé, sent it in with a carefully crafted cover letter, and was delighted to receive an interview request. That day, I met with three different people, so I knew I was a strong candidate. However, the last person made my head spin; he kept snapping his fingers in front of me and saying, "What's the killer app for books, Bethanne? What is it?"

I had no idea. I went home convinced I hadn't gotten the job, and I was right. A couple of weeks later while on vacation with friends, I found a job listing for a big government agency. One of these friends told me I was perfect for the gig, so I applied, but put very little thought into my bona fides. Months went by. Just before Christmas, a man called and asked me to come in to talk about the job I'd applied for during that vacation so many months before. Less than half an hour later, I'd been hired.

Not so fast. I said "big government agency," and the job entailed a big security clearance. More months went by as I excavated former addresses and names of friends and family who had worked as bureaucrats at one time or another. I was willing to wait, because the job was a good one as a writer/editor.

Almost a year to the day after my first call from AOL, I got a second one: The Books Editor position was open again. This time around, I already had a job (*still* pending that clearance), and I was relaxed for the spate of interviews. My cool demeanor paid off because, in a matter of days, I had an offer letter and a start date.

It was a little painful to write a letter turning down the government job, because the woman I would have worked for was terrific—but so was the woman I worked for at AOL. More important, staying with my passion for books, reading, and publishing has brought me many other opportunities. The AOL job lasted just a few years, but it kept me on the path of a lifetime. I've published several books, and I am an active book reviewer and a member of the board of the National Book Critics Circle. I believe that second chances pay off in spades.

—BETHANNE

Saved by Love

I cheated. Or, I am a cheater. Whichever you'd prefer. I guess if you believe the age-old adage "Once a cheater, always a cheater," then it would be the latter.

I did it, that much I can tell you. I own it, I did it. I was soon to turn twenty-four years old, and my heart hadn't been the same since it was broken in college.

Although I hadn't been looking for a relationship, a woman named Chris Ann found me. Through the depression, the anger, the pain, she found me. She saved my life in more ways than I could ever possibly describe. And I almost threw it all away.

My coworkers and I had gathered for a going-away party for one of our managers. Chris Ann and I had recently moved in together, and though she knew that my heart wasn't in it, she persisted and never gave up on me. Sally, a coworker of mine, sent me a text message on the drive in to the bar.

"Are we gonna hook up tonight?" she said.

Perfect opportunity to say, "No." Perfect opportunity to say, "I have a girlfriend." Perfect opportunity to say anything *other* than what I said, which was, "You know it."

I found Sally sitting on a stool near the bar's entrance. I had ample opportunities to choose a different path. But I chose wrong. And that choice has led to the greatest second chance of all. The chance at love.

I lost count of how many shots I took and how many beers I downed, but with each passing hour, Sally moved closer and closer toward me. "When are you taking me home?" she slurred in my ear.

"I'll pay the tab," I stuttered, somehow forming a semi-coherent thought. I drove Sally to her apartment, and I slept with her.

It was a drunken, entirely unsatisfying experience for both of us. I remember standing on her balcony afterward, smoking a cigarette and thinking pretty clearly about throwing myself off the ledge. What was the point of going on living after this?

Chris Ann. She was the point.

I immediately left Sally's apartment to get back to the Bronx. I was driven by a compulsion to confess, to bare my soul. I knew what I had done was wrong even while I was doing it. But I knew, somewhere deep inside, as deep as the Mariana Trench, that I *needed* to tell Chris Ann everything, and immediately.

3:37 A.M. I'll always remember that time. The beginning of the end, or the end of the beginning, depending upon your seat in the room.

"You slept with Sally, didn't you?" Chris Ann said, sitting up in bed and turning on the light, all in one motion.

The truth, never a lie to Chris Ann, not then, and not ever. "Yes. Yes I did. And I'm sorry."

The next several hours, days, were filled with tears. Large

tears that pool at your eyes and fall in great giant heaps to the floor. In the immediate aftermath, Chris Ann was angry, and rightfully so. And then, anger gave way to sadness. The pain I had caused her could never be repaired. And even if, somehow, she could someday forgive me, I didn't think it possible that I would ever be able to forgive myself.

Six years later

The woman I cheated on, the woman I hurt, the woman I almost lost, is now my wife. She saved me, she truly did. I'd never known happiness until I met Chris Ann, and now I know it better than anyone. Every day, even after all of these years, is filled with a love that I can't adequately describe. Chris Ann is the greatest person I've ever met, and I wish the world could know how amazing she is. Every positive adjective in the vocabulary of man applies to her, but none does her justice. She took a depressed, angry, scared boy, and she turned him into a man devoid of fear, filled with happiness and love.

I know I said that she gave me a second chance at love, but it's more than that. She gave me a second chance at life.

—JAMIE

I had ample opportunities to choose a different path. But I chose wrong. And that choice has led to the greatest second chance of all. The chance at love.

Their Separate Ways

Here are the stories of two people (who happen to be my parents) who transformed their lives after life-changing challenges. . . .

My father, Jack, is a recovered alcoholic. In 2016, he marked his forty-sixth year of sobriety. August 16, 1970, was the day he took his last drink, after years of often ugly episodes and, ultimately, a near-death experience the night he truly hit bottom. He is one of those who turned to AA, and for whom it worked. He took a leave from his work as a business and public-relations writer and wrote an autobiographical novel about his years of drinking called *The Morning After*. The book was quite successful and was made into a 1974 TV movie starring Dick Van Dyke. The book and the TV movie are remembered by many as influential in changing their own lives or in recognizing the issues of alcoholism in those close to them.

In the following years, my father wrote half a dozen anonymous day-by-day recovery books, some cowritten with his second wife, Sandy, all aimed at those with issues of addiction, damaged self-esteem, and chronic pain. Most of these books are still in print and have provided guidance, inspiration, and solace to millions of people.

And the counterpoint . . .

My mother, Gloria, was married to my father, Jack, raised three kids with him, and suffered the ravages of his alcoholism. In her early forties, she began working in bookstores in Los Angeles. In October 1974, her husband, who had begun the process of recovering from his alcoholism a few years earlier, left her. She began to take steps that would ultimately transform her life. She was visited by an old friend, her high school gym coach, Rose. She traveled to New York from Los Angeles, where she lived, and upon returning, she told her son that she had gotten a job in a bookstore in Manhattan and would be moving in just a few weeks. Rose had invited her to stay with her until she could find her own place to live.

My mother continued her career in books, eventually becoming the manager of a bookstore and then moving into a publishing house as a salesperson. Over the years, she worked for many large houses and small presses. She specialized in selling books on LGBT, Judaica, and African American issues to traditional and nontraditional outlets. She was known throughout the country for her passion and expertise and undying commitment to the books she sold.

In 1995, twenty years after having moved to New York, my mother had still not moved out of Rose's apartment. On the night before Rose's eighty-ninth birthday, they were joined by Rose's two granddaughters and two of her three kids. After dinner, Rose got into a cab, and when my mother asked her to move in a bit farther, it was clear that Rose had died. Later that evening, my mother told me and one of my sisters that she and Rose had not just been roommates, they had been lovers. She said that our other sister had "forced" her to tell her years before. We had known as well, of course.

Since that time, my mother has been an out and proud advocate for LGBT rights, along with the other issues of equality, peace, and justice that mean so much to her. She still remains the best bookseller I have ever known.

—ANDY

August 16, 1970, was the day
my father took his last drink. . . .
He is one of those who turned to
AA, and for whom it worked.

The Age of Aquarius

I was a terrible typist. I mean just terrible. My mother made me go to summer school during high school and take classes, but it was not a success by any stretch of the imagination. The keys were blank! There were no hints! To this day (many, many years later), I still have to look at the keyboard when I type. I'm looking at the keyboard as I type this!

Obviously, this was all in the days before personal computers, which, if you remember, was not *really* that long ago. So when it came time, just a few years later, to go out with my newly minted sheepskin and find a job, well, I had to know how to type. Especially since I wanted to work in the magazine business; even the men had to know how to type.

So after months of pounding the pavement, I was thrilled to get an interview at a major magazine. I went in, met with what they then called the Man in Personnel, had a chat, and gave him my résumé . . . and then I was asked to take a typing test. All I needed to pass was to type thirty words per minute with maybe just two mistakes, and I would have a chance at this coveted editorial assistant position for the grand sum of $7,500 per annum.

I failed. Badly. Miserably. Tons of errors and maybe eighteen words per minute. How embarrassing! But I guess Ed (the Man in Personnel, who, I would soon learn, always wore the same tie that was really greasy around the knot) saw some promise, and he said I could take the test again if I would go home and practice. I took it again the next week and flunked. Then I begged for one more chance. I remember it was Fourth of July weekend, and I went home to my father's office—where he had an electric typewriter, but no air-conditioning—and typed stuff like, "The quick brown fox jumped over the lazy dog" and stories from the local newspaper for three days. I returned refreshed and eager.

I flunked the third time, but Ed and his greasy tie said that the two people who would be sharing the assistant to be hired still wanted to see me—I guess they liked my résumé for some reason. So I was ushered in to meet them, we talked for a bit, and then they asked me what my sign was. "I'm a triple Leo," I said, and they glanced at each other and nodded. The job was mine. First, second, third chance—it didn't matter. It was the 1970s, baby.

—ALEX

An Artful Change

I retired at fifty-three—twelve years ago. I had spent the better part of my adult life working in a corporate career. My parents had raised me to expect to not have to work to support myself, but rather to get married and raise a family. I had a strong interest in drawing and art as a child and teenager, but was not encouraged to pursue this interest. And I did not get married and have children.

I pursued higher education by taking out student loans and got a degree in the social sciences. After my corporate career ended, I decided that I wanted to pursue my long-dormant creative interests and begin a journey of exploration of the arts. I spent my first summer of retirement at Harvard in the Career Discovery Program, with my focus on landscape design. During that summer, I used a digital camera a great deal, and I developed my photographic eye through the tremendous curriculum and resources I was exposed to at Harvard. My interest in photography became a path on which I had some immediate success: That fall, I was included in a group show in New York City.

Yet, after a few years of doing photography, I became frustrated with the lack of physicality of the process, with the exception of my travels taking landscape photography workshops in remote parts of the United States. So I began to explore other media. I was exposed to the study of encaustic photography, which involves a mixed media use of hot wax with photographs, my own photographs, naturally, as the basis for the finished content. This fascinating medium excited me and continues to be one in which I work. I have also tackled watercolor, acrylics, oils, and assemblage/sculpture, and have discovered what is now my most favorite medium: printmaking. I have made many friends in the art world and have taken many classes and workshops with talented photographers and artists all over the United States. I realize how fortunate I have been to have had the incredible opportunities I have had after my working life, and I try to grab hold of each one wholeheartedly. I don't think that, when I dreamed of my future back in high school, I could ever have imagined pursuing these various horizons and studying and making art like I have the good fortune to do every day. And believe me, I try to make art part of my day every day.

—SANDRA

Making It Legal

After a career as an elementary school teacher and then my stay-at-home years bringing up four children under the age of six, I took paralegal courses simply to get out of the house one night a week. I discovered I LOVED learning the law, and with the encouragement of my professors, at age forty, I decided to go to law school. The kids were still young, so I attended on a part-time basis, and it took me four and a half years to finish. It was never easy, but we survived through chicken pox, car accidents, and grandparent deaths, and with family help, I passed the state bar exam the first time—while battling a stomach flu!

After a brief career as an appellate attorney, I decided to combine my love of law with my passion for education: I now teach, direct academic support efforts, and help law students realize their own dreams of becoming attornies.

Best second career ever!

—ANNE

The Words When There Are None

Years ago, a friend lost her younger sister quite suddenly. I faced the age-old question: What can I possibly say to her? How could anything I say ease her terrible pain? So I procrastinated, and I never called or wrote to her. She lived quite far away, so time passed, and I never had the occasion to see her. Three years went by, and one day, I mentioned my still-guilty conscience to a mutual friend. I felt terrible, because I knew she'd been devastated, and I had done nothing. Our mutual friend simply said, "Write her a note today. It's never too late." I did, with a simple and heartfelt apology, at last expressing my sorrow for her pain.

She was touched and grateful.

Today, we are closer than ever.

—ALAN

"I Can Do This"

I met a wonderful young man in 1980. He was a soldier who had just gotten out of the Israeli Army and was visiting family in the city where I lived. I was a working girl in upstate New York from a very white Anglo-Saxon family. He told me that I had the "spirit of a wild horse," and we fell in love; but after six months, it was time for him to return to Israel. I knew he was a Zionist and I wasn't; he was also only twenty-three and I was twenty-eight, so we went our separate ways, much to my despair.

Fast-forward fourteen years, and I was getting separated from my husband. My Israeli came back, said he never loved anyone else, and we have been together since. I had a tarot card reading in 1995, and my question was: "What is going to happen to my life with M.?" since it seemed to be a huge cliff edge to me. I turned over the card, and it was a man free falling without a parachute and the word "Trust" was below it.

Having faith in your own decisions, strength, and positive energy is everything in making a move as huge as being a non-Jew and moving to the Middle East at a time when the media says everything is horrible and in conflict. Having visited Israel fourteen times, I knew this was not accurate. Between 1999 and 2015, he took me on adventures I would never have attempted (or thought of) on my own. Climbing down gorges

I was frightened of, rappelling off cliffs, hiking places most Israelis have never even seen, swimming through water pools with a backpack over my head. This was the life for me, so I resigned from my jobs, married my beloved husband, and had faith that everything was going to be fine as long as I knew it would be. "I/We can do this, and it is going to be fine" is my daily mantra.

The most surprising side effect of this move is that everyone tells me how brave I am, both in Israel and the United States, when I really just wanted to be with the person I love. The stereotype that one should retire and slow down left with the last generation, I think, since most everyone I know who is retired is busier than ever. It is my moving away from the United States that is the most shocking to everyone. We are told that the United States is the best place in the world to live, that it is number one in everything. But there is a spirit among my Israeli friends that says grab every moment of your life and do something wonderful, meaningful, fun, challenging, whatever, just don't waste it! I love this attitude, and I live it every day. Plus my US family is only a twelve-hour plane flight away, and I have a date to return to see everyone, so I didn't say good-bye, I said, "See you in September!"

—SUSAN

Déjà Vu

I have experienced more second chances in my life than I can count, but a few stand out for the lasting ways that they have shaped me, including the most recent one, in which my wife and I relocated from Cape Cod and her ancestral home by the sea to Western Massachusetts. It was there, years ago, before we even knew each other, that we were both college students nearby. We did what second chances require to be made real: We set a goal to be closer to her daughters and their spouses and our grandchildren, looked for a new home and new jobs, and trusted and relied on the universe to fulfill our vision. Now we find ourselves settling into an old Victorian farmhouse in a hill town off of the Mohawk Trail where we are discovering a whole new life far from the ocean but embraced by the hills, rivers, streams, and forests that surround us.

Sometimes, I think that this second chance I'm experiencing now happened in steps, beginning when I was a twenty-year-old college student, not far from this town I now call home, and I fell in love with my best friend, who was also my college roommate. We called our love a natural extension of our friendship, but as it blossomed and grew, and as I experienced a happiness that made all other joys pale in comparison, I knew I had a deep acceptance to reveal to myself and to my family and friends. I was happy in the arms of my dearest friend because I was a lesbian, but this awareness challenged every Catholic schoolgirl lesson I had been taught. It took courage to come out, because it put me at odds with some of the most important people in my life; it took me to depths of despair that I was not sure I would survive. Coming out allowed me to live an authentic life from which there has been no going back.

Then when I was thirty-two years old, I realized that I was going to need to learn to experience life undiluted by drugs and the liquid courage of alcohol, which I had started using innocently enough as a twelve-year-old, but which I became increasingly dependent on as my life got more complicated. Without daily use of alcohol and marijuana, I was given a chance to live more honestly, and remaining sober over the ensuing years has required vigilance, support, the courage to keep changing, and learning to let go in those times when trusting in a higher power is the best way forward.

My third life-altering change came when I was forty-five years old: My partner and I took the great state of Massachusetts up on its offer to allow same-sex couples to marry. I like to think that we would still be together whether we had married in 2004 or not, but I have to admit that getting married under the law, in our local Unitarian Universalist church, with our family and friends ceremoniously assembled, changed me in ways that I did not expect. Our marriage was a second, deeply personal and yet very public, coming out, and if there were any remnants of self-doubt, self-loathing, or internalized shame, they were vanquished in me that day.

As a married lesbian, I have experienced a self-actualization in love that I wish for everyone—but especially for young gay, lesbian, bisexual, and transgender people who may be questioning their identities.

Last week, as part of my new job, I attended what will be a biweekly staff meeting. When Google Maps announced that I had arrived at my destination, I realized that right next door was a bar that I frequented over forty years earlier when I was a college coed, struggling with my sexuality and completely unaware of the second chances that life would give me.

—BARBARA

Our marriage was a second, deeply personal and yet very public, coming out, and if there were any remnants of self-doubt, self-loathing, or internalized shame, they were vanquished in me that day.

Reunited

I went to work right out of college. As one did. I went to an employment agency with my lovely BA (humanities)—obviously this was pre-Internet job searching! The spinsterish lady at the agency looked through her Rolodex, made a phone call, and sent me out for an interview.

I got a job in sales the next day. I loved it from the start and was promoted quickly.

I worked full-time until my first son was two years old, and then I freelanced for another five years or so, always at the same company, in many departments. In those days, people actually took their two-week vacations, and I would fill in when people's assistants went away. I gained great experience in a variety of departments and loved all of it.

But my husband was working long, long hours, and our children were small, and we moved to a little house in the suburbs. We decided I'd stay home to raise the boys. I loved it. I wasn't a volunteer mom, didn't go in much for committees or school board politics. Instead, I made a wonderful home for our boys (three with just over ten years between them).

I thought I'd be home forever and ticked off the years with no "work" experience. My head was miles from considering working outside our home.

But things changed. My days felt longer and not as fulfilling, and when I had a son who was preparing to go to college, I realized I should make a financial contribution to our household. I'd been away from work for so long, though. I worried whether I was still relevant—if I had anything to offer. I met with the few friends from work I had stayed in touch with. And by "in touch," I mean the occasional e-mail, the long-awaited drink date. I tried not to feel discouraged by how much time had passed. I hoped someone would give me a chance.

Someone did. In July, I met with a man I had worked with more than a decade earlier. He gave me a chance to state my case. His assistant wasn't really working out, and he asked me if I'd like to start after Labor Day. Though it didn't seem like a life-changing moment at the time, it definitely turned out to be just that.

Having a job, getting a job at my age, was a wonderful thing. I've made myself an indispensable member of a team, something I hadn't really done before. Because my children are grown, I've had all the time and energy I've needed to start my career again. I was given, and then earned, another opportunity in the working world, and I am terrifically grateful.

—MERLE

Learning from Spectacular Failure

I am a serial entrepreneur. By definition, that vocation requires incredible resilience. Quite frankly, joining this unique club also requires that you meet and recognize failure as a teacher.

While there have been other failures in my career and in my personal life, the one that has set me up for the second chance that I am living right now was what I call my "spectacular failure." I wear it as a badge of courage; after all, I have earned that right.

At age forty-nine, after eleven years of having my own strategic consulting firm, I raised over $7 million for my first entrepreneurial venture.

Not bad, you say. Well, $7 million seems like a lot, until you realize that you need $10 million to get past launch and to retool from the early learning and then sign your next major client(s), and then lather, rinse, and repeat until you break even.

The company's name was LeisureLogix, and we were building B2B (business-to-business) technology for the road-travel market. We had everything right, or so I thought (famous last words . . .).

In short, the market is humongous. That is, bigger than big. Our launch client was the number two online travel agency in the world. We hired the dream team to lead the way forward. And I had found an angel investor who put in the majority of the money.

We were in hog heaven. We had a dedicated team who had worked together for a number of years, and many of whom had worked for many months on this venture for sweat equity.

But less than forty-five days after launch, after getting that coveted *Wall Street Journal* article and winning a prestigious innovator of the year award at a top industry conference, the dream ended. From idea to build to launch to shutdown was just over fifteen months. In entrepreneurial circles, that is called failing fast.

My investor lost $6 million, and my husband and I lost nearly $1 million. Not that we ever "had" $1 million. Through this whole experience, I learned the word "leverage" was more than an engaging television series. We put everything on the line. And we lost.

But we rolled the dice. Some people never get to do that. And trust me, it is a thrill. If it wasn't, we wouldn't become serial entrepreneurs!

Now I am twenty-four months into my latest tech start-up venture. This time, I am self-funding. I am tackling the 67 percent of travel that is NOT vacation and is NOT business travel—those trips that are so often for a single life event, like a concert, funeral, volunteer opportunity, college-hunting. And we contribute 10 percent of our revenues to the charity of choice of each client. We are changing the world, one trip at a time.

I still have sleepless nights when I wonder how I am going to make it (note I am beyond wondering "if" I will make it), but every day I wake up praying for peace and clarity of vision, and my provider is faithful to his promises on all fronts.

Failing fast? This time I'd rather not fail at all. And I won't. Just watch!

—CHICKE

Our Father's Suicide

I'd traveled to a mental health center in Maryland to do a presentation about how to cope with the loss of a loved one to suicide. The facility was a short drive from where my brother and sister live, so it shouldn't have surprised me when they both decided to attend—even though, beyond acknowledging the fact of it, we'd never discussed that our father killed himself.

As the author of a book on suicide, I'd rarely hesitated to share my story—how deeply traumatized I'd been, how I'd spent years seeing a therapist and still did, even talking about how my siblings and I had never truly spoken about what happened. For more than four decades, we'd each been on our own private journeys. Now, our paths were about to converge.

I could have asked Heidi and Lewis to stay away, explaining that it would be too emotional for me to have them there, but a part of me loved the idea of having their support. What I hadn't counted on was that in a room filled with more than a hundred mental health professionals, they'd take second-row seats, in my direct line of sight. I could not help looking at them as I began to share—at first with all the assuredness of a seasoned expert—what I'd come to think of as my story alone.

The phone rang on a wintry Sunday morning in 1970. It was my father's sister-in-law. I handed the phone to my mother, and within seconds, she ushered me out of the kitchen, closing the door firmly behind me. Ever the curious twelve-year-old, I listened through the door's keyhole. "It took two words—'pills' and 'hospital'—for me to discern the truth," I told the audience. "My dad died three days later. The official cause of death: pneumonia."

It was impossible to miss the tears rolling down my sister's cheeks. As I finished telling my story, I was startled by the realization that I had no idea when or how she learned the truth. With my brother, I vaguely recalled that I was the one who had accidentally set the record straight when we were in college, but my recollection was mostly vapor.

"Heidi," I said, gently locking eyes with my sister, "I have no idea how you found out what happened to Dad." I looked at my brother, whose eyes were wet, and choked up, thinking to myself, "'Dad'—that's a word I've hardly ever said to the two of you."

I stared down at my notes and wiped the tears from my face. I looked up at the audience; some were wiping away tears themselves.

"Rather than conduct a family therapy session in a roomful of therapists," I told them with a half smile, "I think Heidi, Lewis, and I will continue this conversation tomorrow over breakfast." The tension dissolved into laughter. I went on with my presentation, offering advice on how to help suicide loss survivors with their healing journeys, but now with the façade of authority stripped away.

The next morning, my brother, sister, and I sat down

for the first time to talk about our father's suicide—what we knew when, how we felt then, how we'd integrated that loss into our lives. Nothing could undo the damage inflicted by our father's death at his own hands, but sharing in that experience for the first time, we had the chance to heal the ancient breach that had left us to struggle with that reality on our own.

—ERIC

Yours, Mine, and Ours

How were we to know an amazing second chance would begin that ordinary day on a bus in Japan?

The years have dulled the name of the city, but it was on a long bus ride at the end of a long day toward the end of a long trip to Japan, required to complete our MBA. We were very similar, she and I: We were both young—in age, in career experience, and in our respective marriages. As our education was coming to an end, it would soon be time for a new chapter in our lives—one with very little sleep and very tiny socks and lots of crying (both from our babies and, sometimes, the mamas). We talked about motherhood on that bus ride, and when we walked into the football stadium at Ohio State University on a blindingly hot day in June to graduate, we each brought a plus one with us underneath our robes.

Millions of women in the United States give birth each year, but even in modern-day America, with amazing medical science, sometimes things don't go as planned. Thankfully, my friend had a healthy baby, but it was after a petrifying medical emergency that she herself almost didn't survive. And this amazing mom—one of those moms who has a crazy challenging corporate job, travels nonstop yet still bakes homemade cookies for teacher appreciation day the midnight before, and is the Girl Scout leader, and most amazingly

HAS A KID WHO LOVES TO EAT VEGETABLES—was left unable to carry another baby.

Nine years later, after me (alarmingly casually, really) blurting out, "Oh, I've always thought about being a surrogate mom," and her saying, "Are you serious?" and after months of very serious discussions, my husband and I sat our kids down on the couch and said, "We have a family decision to make." And after that conversation, we told our old friends that we would love to provide a warm, safe home for their child for nine months.

Having a baby via science is mind-boggling and involves crazy medicines and shots and schedules . . . and one really smart doctor who hugged me before she took one teeny embryo out of a freezer and gave me the opportunity to tell people I was pregnant but "it's not my husband's baby. Or mine."

On the eleventh of August, 2015, in a hospital in Minnesota, a sweet little cherub made her way into the world. While she doesn't share my DNA, I like to think she got her love of guacamole and a really super laugh from her time with me. While it was a second chance for my friend to complete the family she always wanted, I think it gave our family even more. Sometimes, the happy ending to the story takes a few more years than you intended—but I am thrilled to know there is a tangible representation of love and friendship running around Arizona in a sundress today, chasing her puppy dog and hugging her big sister. And she is the best second chance ever.

—MELISSA

Yours, Mine, and, Finally, Ours

I married my high school sweetheart when I was in my early twenties. We were true soul mates and best friends. We had two boys eighteen months apart. Our life was centered around family. He was a very involved dad; we spent countless hours at soccer fields, baseball fields, and just hanging out as a family. When our boys were eight and ten, and he and I were just thirty-seven years old, my husband died unexpectedly—on the day of my youngest son's communion.

I remember knowing that my mission in life was to raise my sons to be good people and not being afraid to do that alone. I did not embrace dating; I was fearful of falling in love and getting hurt again. I know that part of grieving is to be angry, but I was not angry at my husband—it wasn't his choice to leave us so soon. I wasn't angry except when I was on a date! Because, eventually, I would accept a night out—nights I referred to as "dates from hell"—and through the entire evening, I would be mad at my late husband for putting me through this!

Then a friend asked me if I would go on a blind date. I had never done that before, but her friend was a widower with three daughters, and that intrigued me. I met Mark for a drink, and it was the first date since my husband passed away where I actually had fun!

Mark and I had a lot in common, and we were both quite spontaneous. We dated for two years and at last made the major decision to bring our families together. Our kids were a freshman, sophomore, junior, and senior in high school and a fourth grader. We had to be crazy! But we both sold our houses and bought one large home where there was plenty of private space and common space. Bringing teenage children together had its challenges for sure.

We have just celebrated twenty years together. Our children are all out of college and the last wedding is this fall. We have two grandchildren and hope for many more. What we did was risky and probably one of the hardest things I've ever done, but it is also one of the most rewarding. Our kids remain close and refer to one another as brothers and sisters—something I don't think either of us could have expected. I learned that life offers more chances if you just open your eyes and heart to them.

—JANE

Telephone

Long, long ago, at the dawn of the World Wide Web, the Internet helped me lose my job. I worked at a big-city newspaper, and though we weren't really using e-mail yet, we did have an early version of interoffice electronic communication. I sent a note to someone in the office and made a comment about how I thought my boss would react to a situation at hand. "Jack's going to have a cow!" I e-wrote my cohort. The problem is, I hit what was later to become known as the "Reply All" button, and everyone in the newsroom got the message. Good-bye, job.

I thought it was a little harsh—after all, it was an honest, if naïve, mistake—but a couple of weeks after I got sacked, I happened to hear *exactly* how I lost my job from a friend. Remember the old game Telephone, where everyone whispered a message to the person next to them in a circle, and then everyone laughed, astonished when you heard what came out at the other end? Well, this was the best round of Telephone ever. My friend called me and asked about the firing. "Did you really say, 'The princess stamped his tiny foot'?" It was so funny that it took a lot of the edge off the firing. And if that's what I had *really* said, I would have fired me, too!

Don't wait for the part of this story where I get that job back, because I did not. But I got another chance elsewhere in the industry, moved on to the next step in my career, and frankly, never looked back, though it was a rough spot at the time. And over the years, I also—thankfully—became much more technologically proficient.

—BILL

Road Trip

In March of 2015, at the age of fifty-five and at the end of a fifteen-year relationship, I realized I was trying to figure out what I would do, could do, next in my life. There is a saying, "Analysis leads to paralysis," and I was certainly stuck.

I had been a lifelong singer, songwriter, troubadour. The last decade and a half had afforded me the opportunity to not worry about how to make money with my art, but to seek out ways to inspire (hence my performing in the subways, bringing music into public spaces, and donating my performances for not-for-profit events). The music industry terrain had completely shifted due to the Internet age, and now I had to support myself and my two standard poodles, Etta and Lily. I didn't know if any chance of a career in music was over or if I should consider a new direction based on all the skills I had learned over my life or learn new ones. The only solution I found was to leap into the idea that I couldn't yet answer the question of what to do next. I thought of a favorite childhood John Steinbeck book, *Travels with Charley*, and an idea was born: to take a road trip with the poodles.

I packed up my personal belongings, put some into a small storage space, got rid of things I didn't need. What kind of car? I didn't want a camper or anything too big, so I settled on a Prius v wagon. There was enough room for the pups in the way back, and the backseat was big enough for the things I would need for a trip of an indefinite time—certainly guitars and my busking equipment were necessary, but also seasonal clothes.

I had lived in Key West in the 1980s and Paris, France, in the 1990s—why not consider a new place to live? I started out from New York City. I barely made any kind of itinerary except to know I wanted to head north, then west, and drive counterclockwise around the country like a board game. I knew I had to have a budget, but I didn't want to obsess with the spending. Realistically and carefully composting my savings into fertile soil to sow needed seeds of growth in my life seemed a worthwhile investment. To continue metaphorically, if I was a fine sweater I had knitted my whole life, during my trip, I would slowly unravel it until I ended up with a huge ball of yarn ready to create a new me.

We left September 23, the first day of autumn. In the end, we traveled 180 days, drove 18.330 miles, slept in 60 different beds (one cold night in the car in Big Sur), and visited 29 states.

People say that I'm courageous. I am not so sure I think so; anyone can do what I have done. I took this trip to be self-preserving. What this journey did do was inspire me. And it gave me the courage to see a future full of possibility.

—CATHY

Turnaround

I'm telling the story of my friend, whom I'll call John, because he can't tell it himself.

When I met him, we were in our late teens, early twenties, and, of course, lots of us in our crowd were still working at jobs, not careers, trying to figure out what came next . . . or hoping someone would tell us, I suppose. What John did was sell drugs. Big quantities, scary quantities, and whatever type of stuff he could get his hands on, from weed to pills and probably plenty of things I don't even want to know about.

The weird thing was, though, that John was loving and kind and trustworthy. Protective of his friends. The nicest guy you'd ever want to know. Because we loved him, we all hoped he'd get out of the drug-dealing business, because we didn't want anything bad to happen to him. On the other hand, we were really young, and we assumed nothing would.

One night, John was driving back home from up north, where he had made a sizable purchase of drugs, which, of course, were in the car with him. Twice, he was stopped by the police on the way home—routine stops; he had done nothing wrong, as far as his driving was concerned. I guess he just looked suspicious in some way because the second cop asked if he could look inside the trunk of John's car. That's where the drugs were. John had no choice and acquiesced, but miraculously the police decided not to open it.

I guess it was the sign—or kick in the pants—John needed, because he never sold drugs again. That night, he called it quits. He went on to get a regular job—well, perhaps not *that* regular. John works for the government, has a high security clearance, and spends his days protecting people like you and me from cybercrime. He put on the white hat and never looked back. I can't speak to what made him do what he did— and by that I mean both choose to sell drugs or work for the US government—but to me it proves he just grew into the wonderful, caring man I always knew he was. And it speaks to the fact that a lot of kids are not yet the grown-ups they can become, and sometimes, they just need to figure it out for themselves. John came very close to not having his second chance, but when he grabbed it, he held on.

—ON MY FRIEND "JOHN"

"Girls Like You"

Back when I was in high school, in the late 1960s, you had one chance to go see the guidance counselor to discuss your future and talk about what colleges you might hopefully get into. I went to a Catholic high school, so, naturally, our guidance counselor was a nun.

She had it in for me from the start; I was a smart enough student, but she had formed an opinion of me a long time before. I smoked cigarettes. I flirted with boys. Maybe I wore my plaid school uniform skirt a little too short for her taste. This was my one shot, and I have to admit, I was feeling a little uneasy.

She had an opinion, all right. "Girls like you should be dental assistants," she said. That was it; I was summarily dismissed, and any thoughts I had of college were pretty much gone with the wind.

I thank her now, though.

Many years later—in fact, I was forty-two—I gained the confidence to go to college, and the disservice she did me still hurt. So when it came time for me to go for my master's in special education, and it came time to write my thesis, I had a title ready: "Girls Like You." It was about all the ways that educators influence students.

When I finished graduate school, I did not become a dental assistant. I became a teacher. I believe my kids respect me, and they know that they can come to me about almost anything. Not at all the outcome Sister saw for me—but perhaps she got me there, in spite of herself.

—DENISE

Forgiveness

After twenty-five years of marriage to a wonderful man, I knew without a doubt that I wanted and needed to ask his first wife for forgiveness. The details of our courtship, wedding, and family are not important; what is important is that I had fallen in love with a married man who then experienced a painful divorce and married me shortly thereafter. I welcomed his two young children into our lives, and soon we had two of our own children. Needless to say, my husband's first wife was furious with me, angry with her ex-husband, and very sad. I kept busy and made every attempt to be pleasant and kind whenever our paths crossed, but I never apologized. Perhaps because my husband also harbored intense anger about his first marriage, I did not want to rock the boat and betray him by asking for forgiveness from his first wife.

As the years passed, I became more and more aware of God working in my life. I studied the Bible, attended church regularly, and made it clear to my family that God was an important presence in our household. And I kept asking God for guidance. During a large extended family celebration in our home one warm spring afternoon, my husband's first wife and I happened to be in the same room alone together, and I gently approached her and said, "I would like to ask for your forgiveness." I think she was as surprised as I was.

Although I had been thinking about doing this for a long time, I had not planned the time and place. But, there we were, together, and I simply spoke. She said that she would call me and we would talk.

That was eight years ago, and in the time since, we have had some powerful and very personal conversations. And while we do not converse often, I am no longer wracked with guilt when I see her at family events. We chat about our children and grandchildren; we worry about many of the same things; we have given each other a second chance. And every Ash Wednesday, she calls me to say she remembers our forgiveness, and I tell her that her call means the world to me.

—PAULINE

What's Next?

The confluence of my midsixties (the traditional age to think about retirement) and a serious, usually fatal illness caused me to assess my priorities and my plan for the rest of my life (or, at least, the next few years). The result isn't really a change, but rather a turning-up of a part of my life that, prior to this point, played a minor role and the simultaneous turning-down of another part (my professional life) that previously occupied a large majority of my time.

So I'm doing less of one thing, more of another. And I had the chance to figure that out as a plan and then do it.

—BRIAN

Never Say Never

In 1969, I returned to my beloved childhood summer camp as a counselor. I was seventeen—the youngest member of the staff—had no particular training, and was housed in a small cabin by myself with no mentor or even a friend. I loved my campers and found a little success teaching tennis, but I slogged through the summer feeling lonely and inadequate. I never made it back for another summer.

Never, that is, until the job as camp director was advertised in 2003. For a whole host of reasons, this seemed like a perfect opportunity for me. After twenty-five years of teaching English, I was delighted at the thought of not grading papers, and my personal life was in some turmoil. Time for a change. And now I could go back and do it again. I could do it right this time—and help others to do it right the first time. I applied for the position, and I got the job.

My twelve years as director there renewed my love of my summer camp, brought me back to a simple lifestyle, reminded me of the value of play, and allowed me to work with countless young women in their roles as camp counselors. Giving them the resources and training that they needed became one of my major priorities, and second chances were very much a part of that. I knew what it felt like to lack confidence and lack support. A nineteen-year-old who makes a mistake does not need to be sent packing, but needs to be allowed to try again—in fact, is required to do so.

I cannot fathom what I would have missed if I had not taken this second chance. I learned as much from a nine-year-old away from home for the first time as I did from the traditions and values that are the foundation of camp. What I want to know is: Where are the camps for grown-ups?

—ANNE

Anne has now retired from the camp that gave her so much joy as a camper (not so much as counselor) and director. This is a letter from one of her counselors, written to her at the close of her last summer at the camp. . . .

Dear Mrs. C.

I hope you don't think that because this is your last summer as director, we'll forget about your other wonderful years at this camp. Especially me. I've had the blessing of your great leadership and guidance for the majority of my camper years and beyond. Whether you knew it already or not, you have left a great impact on my life. What I am most grateful for, and is one of the greatest things you have taught me, is the ability to give second chances. No matter our mistakes, you give second chances and forgive with grace. With that you've given me the chance to forgive myself in times I've made the wrong choice or a mistake. From those moments you have helped me grow into a stronger, more thoughtful woman. You dealt with me as a candy-eating camper in the most challenging cabin group, to a klutzy camper with an eye patch . . . you always accepted me back: something I will forever be grateful for. Directly and indirectly you have taught me to keep trying, never give up, how to be a strong person mentally and physically, how to challenge myself, how to listen, how to lead . . . and the list goes on forever. Your years as director may be coming to a close, but you'll forever have an impact on all our lives.

Love always,
Chealsey

The Best Thing That Ever Happened

Ever since I had started working after college, I had heard the age-old saying from many a career veteran: "When I got laid off, it was the best thing that ever happened to me." Well, when *I* was laid off in 2008, I sorely begged to differ! I had worked in book publishing for over a decade, and I was attached to not only the job, but also the industry itself—it was part of my identity. So losing my job was devastating to me—I cried and raged for several months, lashing out at both family and friends. And try as I might, I could not find another job, either in publishing or anywhere else for that matter. So I took the time to do some soul-searching, and while the path was not linear (I had a few missteps along the way), I decided to go back to school to get my master's in social work, specifically so that I could work with the senior population. Changing careers and being back in school with twentysomethings while I was in my late thirties was no easy matter for me, but now that I'm a social worker in a nursing home, I know I found my calling. Of course, you could not have told me that eight years ago! Book publishing will always be my first love, but to be able to pursue a second career that I find tough, yes, but emotionally satisfying, really is the *best thing that ever happened to me.*

—ANNE

Second Time Around

I practically ran away from my college graduation in May of 1998 to move to New York City and begin living the dream of being a city dweller. I was young, entertaining a handful of first job offers, and hungry to explore the city. It was a wonderful moment of feeling alive and free.

I spent my twenties in the city as many do: living in tiny apartments, choosing a night out over sleep, and frequently learning my lesson about the importance of budgeting money in this expensive metropolis.

This first affair with NYC lasted about eight years, and for the most part, it was a blur of wonderful memories. I remember concerts at the Roseland Ballroom and Irving Plaza, getting close to celebrities like David Sedaris at Shakespeare & Co. in SoHo (now a Foot Locker), even sitting in front of Kevin Kline and Phoebe Cates at my first Broadway show (*The Scarlet Pimpernel*!). I was in an all-girl band, Boobytrap, and got to live out my rock-star dreams for a time.

There were dark moments, too. I was robbed at gunpoint. September 11 unfolded before my eyes. On that morning, I was briefly caught in the shadow of the first plane as I walked to work. And then, from a rooftop on 19th Street, I watched the towers break apart. That day was never-ending and horrifying, and it left an indelible mark on my head and heart.

Just a few years later, my relationship with the city started changing. It was a confusing time. By 2005, the band had broken up. Suddenly, there was more free time and less routine. Other things started shifting: jobs ended, relationships unraveled. I felt stuck, even a bit trapped. How was it that this place of possibility and promise suddenly felt like a dead end? It hurt to think that everything I worked so hard for left me feeling alone and misguided. I faced the ultimate Clash moment: "Should I stay or should I go?" And the bigger question: If I went, would I ever return?

I did leave, and after three years in L.A., I did return. Why? It felt necessary to go back to where I felt most alive. Truthfully, I couldn't stop thinking about the city my entire time away. Three years and three thousand miles felt like the right combination to gain perspective. Not surprisingly, I felt transformed—older, wiser. Now I had a much better sense of self, and a much clearer idea of how to love this city and get it to love me back. It was personally enriching to leave and then return as the person I always was, only better.

In some way, I always knew New York would be where I made my life. Though it still does break my heart on occasion, it provides and fulfills where I need it most. My intentions with the universe felt heard the year I returned, and in one fell swoop, I landed a dream job, married a dreamboat, and gave birth to a dream child. Finally, New York and I had an understanding of how my life here could be. It just took time and space to get there.

—CHRISTINA

Bounceback

My part-time position at a top-tier college was eliminated last year. This has been a tough time for me, as I had worked there for over thirteen years. I am an undergrad and graduate alumna of the school. My husband still works there, so my ties are deep.

About six months before my job elimination, I decided that I was not getting any younger and that I needed to pursue a career path that I had been thinking about for years. I had spoken to several in the field over the years, and they had dissuaded me from the transition because of my young kids and our family's need for consistent income. Regardless, I took the leap and enrolled in the real estate salesperson class at a local real estate school. I had to ask a lot of favors from people in my life in order to take this class. It ran from 8:00 A.M. until 5:00 P.M. My position at the college was still part-time, so I was the one responsible for getting the kids to school and getting them off the bus at the end of their day. During the three-week course, one of the weeks was February vacation for the kids. My mother-in-law flew in from Washington to watch the kids while I made the half-hour trip to and from class each day. We asked a neighbor friend to take the kids to school a few days during the three weeks my class was going on and lined up babysitters to get the kids after school for those days. I took vacation days and worked extra days after the class to make up the time lost at the college. Sometimes, I think this is the real heart of this story—I never would have had the opportunity to even try this without the team of folks who helped me get through those *loooong* three weeks.

The course ended, and I took the state real estate license test—and I passed! I started work at a local realty office and began training—still all around my part-time schedule at the college. About six weeks after I had taken the test for my real estate license, I was called into a meeting: The college had decided to eliminate my small department in a realignment and reallocation of resources. I was scared, thankful, relieved, mad, and happy all at the same time. I started showing houses and offering to cover open houses for other agents. The timing seemed almost miraculous—somehow I had started pursuing my new career just in time.

It has been almost a year now, and it has been the hardest and best year of my life. Yes, it's been stressful—especially when I don't know when I will next get paid—but at this moment, I have three transactions due to close soon, which is exciting for me personally and professionally—and of course from a personal budget perspective.

I know that I will never do anything else job-wise, and I am happy to have found one that I love—it doesn't even feel like a job because I get so much enjoyment from it.

—KIRSTIN

Sunshine

A few years ago, I lost a job that I really loved. Then, a few weeks after that, I lost the home that I had lived in for thirty years to a fire. I found myself basically homeless with two teenage daughters. My husband had to go live with his mother for several months, and we almost lost our marriage. My best friend and her husband allowed us to use her son's bedroom so we wouldn't have to sleep in a shelter. I couldn't imagine anything worse.

After the initial shock wore off and the sun came up again the next day, and then the next day, and the next day, I began to count my blessings, mainly that I had not lost one family member in that fire. Things can be replaced. I applied for a job, and the very next week, they called me in to work! Soon after that, I got a new apartment, and the four of us could be together again.

I'm still standing. The sun still rises every day and problems still come up. Every day I shake the dust off my feet and keep it movin'. I'm striving to get back more than I lost—mostly, peace and stability. God is still good!

—AIISHA

The Last-Minute Hire

When I was seventeen, I was admitted to a wonderful college and given a full academic scholarship. I had never even seen this school because we couldn't afford to make the four-hour trip for an interview. And despite the scholarship, I still had the cost of room and board and books plus spending money to earn before September. Unfortunately, despite their enthusiasm, my family was in no position to assist me financially. I had a great job teaching tennis in the summer, and could pick up additional private lessons to supplement my paycheck, but it still was clear that this would only get me halfway there.

I was walking on the beach on a cold spring day after my acceptance, grappling with the problem. No matter how I looked at it, I'd never get to go to this great school that had offered me so much. There was no way I'd get enough money to cover my expenses by September. Heartily disappointed, I was resigned to telling the school I couldn't come. As I trudged through the sand, I ran into the son of one of my mother's friends. A decade older than I, and hopelessly handsome and sophisticated to my seventeen-year-old eyes, he kindly stopped to talk. He cheered my college choice and saw through my attempt to cover up how desperate I was to find a high-paying job to make this work.

"Why don't you go down to the Bell Buoy and tell Bob, the owner, that Freddy thinks you'd make a good waitress for him for the summer."

It took me a day to gather my courage to go to the most popular restaurant in town. Everyone knew their waitresses made great money because they worked year-round, and besides, they were famous for their experience and good looks. Only a few lucky girls were hired in the summer to accommodate the beach crowd. Even I knew that a skinny, braces-wearing, inexperienced applicant who wouldn't even be old enough to serve alcohol until the upcoming Fourth of July didn't have a prayer.

Still, I walked into the boss's office to ask for a summer job. I focused on my willingness to work and learn, since I had no other credentials. He looked me up and down and told me he was sorry, he had no openings. As I was leaving, in a supreme act of courage, I said, "Freddy thought you might need someone." He looked up. I held my breath. Was this man going to—somehow, impossibly—rethink his decision? "Freddy sent you?" It seemed like he was trying to decide if this was his friend's idea of a practical joke or if Freddy was serious about giving me a chance. "I'll tell you what, I'll give you a try," he said.

I was a terrible waitress (a pizza actually slipped off my tray onto someone's lap one night), but I was a really hard worker. I would volunteer for unwanted shifts. I would run errands for the bartenders and take the worst customers and the sections everyone else avoided. I'd change from my tennis clothes into my uniform in the restaurant bathroom. I worked seven days a week.

I made my school payments. I worked at the Bell Buoy every summer throughout college. And even though I thanked Freddy later on, he still has no idea how much he helped by giving me the chance I so needed.

—DANA

My Life's Dream

When I was in fourth grade, my teacher asked me to get up and read my composition before the class; I had gone beyond the original assignment and written a little story—it had a beginning, middle, and very action-packed ending, and I was really excited about it. I finished my recitation, and the entire class erupted into applause. Unheard of! My first thought was, "Oh, this is for me." Telling stories, everyone rapt: That was the moment I knew I wanted to be a writer.

I spent a couple of decades, mostly happy ones, as an advertising creative director, but the subject at hand was always someone else's product. When I wasn't doing that, I was partying too hard. Those days ended, and when I'd finally gotten myself together, my first thought was, "I'm tired of writing about everybody else's stuff. I'm going to write my own books."

So at the age of fifty-two, I got a part-time job and started out again. I've written books large and small, and I've published more than twenty-five of them. It's really hard, and the money is not like the old advertising days, but it's just what I always dreamed of. I'm an author.

—ERIN

Just One Year . . .

As I approached the age of sixty-two, I began to realize that I had been doing pretty much the same thing professionally (marketing and public relations) since I was twenty-five. I was enjoying it less—and doing it less successfully. I considered alternatives, but they all seemed like variations on the same tune. Then, one day, a friend suggested that I think about teaching English in a foreign country. I looked into it on the Internet and became hooked on the idea of trying it— for one year only—just to regroup, recharge, and reconsider what I should *really* do next. Thirty days after my first online search, my co-op was rented, my belongings were in storage, and my flight was preparing to land in China.

Now, ten years later, I'm still in China, with a new partner, new family, new friends, a new and beautiful apartment, new dogs, and best of all, a new career that provides me with greater satisfaction than I ever experienced in my US life. There is much I miss about America, but I've never felt a moment of longing or regret. I've learned that change, while initially fearful, opens opportunities previously unimaginable. This is indeed a "second—and late-arriving—act," and while I do not imagine a third, neither do I count it out. It's never too late for another "act."

—TOM

This is indeed a "second—and late-arriving—act," and while I do not imagine a third, neither do I count it out. It's never too late for another "act."

Hello, Old Friend

Nearly a decade ago, a job promotion for my husband meant he had to commute from Boston to spend part of each week in New York City. I was able to shift my schedule to join him for a weekly overnight in the city, and I decided to embrace the opportunity to learn more about museums and theatre in a city I didn't know very well. Then I realized that I also could use this time as a chance to reconnect with a dear college friend who lived in the city, and whom I had barely seen in decades. Happily, she was equally delighted to renew our friendship. So every Thursday morning, I would walk the fifteen blocks to a diner near her apartment, and for an hour, we would laugh until we cried and solve the problems of our families and the world. I was reminded of why this funny, vital woman with an indomitable and generous spirit had become a dear friend in the first place. When both our schedules accommodated, we would explore the quirky and fun oddities found, as they say, "only in New York." It reframed what was often a grueling five-year commute to New York as an extraordinary opportunity and a gift of rekindled friendship.

—SUSAN

Sticking It Out

I had just started the tenth grade at a new school. Up to that point, I had always received excellent grades on my report cards. I liked school, and I think I was actually a nerd.

And then, suddenly, I was in an American history class with Mr. M. On the first quiz, I received a C, and I almost flunked the next one. I truly didn't understand why. I had studied the material as always and thought I knew it. Mr. M.'s comments were that I was just stringing facts together and not really thinking about the hows and whys.

I was not happy about it—in fact, I was mad. I didn't want this class to ruin my grade average, so I tried to switch out and get assigned to another teacher. Well, I couldn't, so I just had to keep going to that class and trying to figure it out.

And that is the best thing that could have happened. I really believe that in Mr. M.'s course, I truly learned to analyze and not just memorize. I know now that he also helped me become a much better writer.

In the end, I did OK in the course and went on to take another course with Mr. M. In retrospect, he had a great deal to do with my success in high school, and then college, and gifted me with my love for writing in general. I still owe Mr. M. a big thank-you; I kept at it, and he stayed with me.

—CARLA

After the Fall

On January 5, 1999, in Vail, Colorado, my life was to change forever.

I was an accomplished skier, taking a beginner lesson in snowboarding with my wife, Joanna. The day was sunny and cold. The conditions were icy. As I made a first attempt at a turn on the board, I caught an edge and ricocheted backward. In those days, no one wore helmets. My head hit the ice, and as I stood up, I thought to myself that the impact had been very dramatic. As the day wore on, a headache began, and it was like nothing I had ever experienced. But I ignored it. Then, believe it or not, I had to take Joanna to the hospital for a broken wrist, which had also happened during our fateful lesson. The headache became worse. I *still* tried to ignore it. We finally went back to our condo, where I took some Advil and had a glass of wine. I would later learn this was the worst thing I could have done.

The next day, I went out again with a ski instructor/friend. I fell again and had trouble getting up. My friend called the paramedics, and the next thing I knew, I was rapidly en route to the hospital, having to answer questions that would continue to be asked of me for several days. Things like, "What's your name?" "Who is the president?" "Where do you live?" "How old are you?"

As they wheeled me into the emergency room, I finally realized the severity of my condition. After a CAT scan, I heard the technician saying, "We've got a bleeder!" I asked the doctor if they were referring to me and if I was critical. He responded "Yes" to both. I felt myself going into shock and asked for blankets. As I lay in the hospital emergency room, I suddenly felt a strong pull upward. I opened my eyes and saw a lovely white light and experienced a very calming and beautiful feeling of serenity. I suddenly realized I might be dying and began a fight that would last for weeks to come. The story goes on with a terrible snowstorm and no way to get a helicopter in to take me to a Denver hospital, as the one in Vail has no head trauma unit. A three-hour trip to Colorado Springs, during which I had to keep talking to make sure I was conscious, followed. Ultimately, I was medevaced to New York City and was lucky enough to meet a neurologist who saved my life. As far as I know, I have recovered completely. My appreciation and gratitude for life has become far deeper. I took a drawing class and began to notice details I had never been aware of. My love for my family steered my course, and I tell them daily how much I love them. It was a traumatic injury and a long and painful recovery. Surviving the ordeal has given me a life filled with curiosity, astonishment, and appreciation on a profound level.

And if you're wondering, YES, I went back to ski and snowboard the next year, and I've gone every year since. The injury never slowed me down, but now the whole family wears helmets. I still believe two things:

FASTER IS BETTER.

And what Bob Dylan said:

"Yes, to dance beneath the diamond sky with one hand waving free."

—OLIVE

Congratulations . . . Again!

Like most of us, I was invited to a lot of weddings in my twenties. At a few of them, I did not give a gift, and I still feel guilty about it. Now, thirty years later, I feel it is too late . . . or is it? What should I send?

At this point, they surely have all the flatware and gadgets one collects over the years. So for my second chance, I am going to send each couple a gift certificate to a restaurant in their city in honor of their next anniversary with a note that says, "Thank you for including me on your wedding day; in honor of your years together, have dinner on me."

—TIM

Life After Life

I have been given two second chances in life, and for that, I consider myself very lucky.

When I was eleven years old, I became very ill with an autoimmune disease that ravaged much of my body and resulted in two different emergency helicopter rides from my local community hospital to a major medical center. The first second chance comes into play during this period. My brilliant doctor and the team of nurses at Boston Children's Hospital saved my life, on multiple occasions. Spending the majority of my first semester of middle school in the hospital guided my career interests from a goal of being an Olympic swimmer to a firm plan to be a nurse. My goal was to be just like the nurses who were there for me throughout my stay; at the morning med pass, while I was incredibly bored at 2:30 P.M., and when I was in incredible pain at 2:30 A.M., they were patient and kind, smart and confident. By saving my life, the nurses gave me a second chance to be just like them. I applied only to colleges with excellent nursing schools, and after graduating from high school, and surviving a few more minor health blips, I was on my way to one of the top nursing schools in the country.

My *second* second chance came about fifteen years later. I had defeated the autoimmune disorder back in middle school, but my kidneys were significantly damaged by the disease. Though I remained in fair health and appeared completely healthy to those who did not know me, my kidneys were on a slow decline. By the time I graduated from college and began my first nursing job, my kidneys were operating only at approximately 20 percent. My renal team at Children's began to make preparations for a transplant so that I could continue to work at the job I loved. I am so lucky to have incredibly supportive family and friends; many stepped up to be donors. It turned out that the best match was my younger sister, and though she was only twenty-two years old at the time, she heroically gave up her kidney to save my life.

I healed well and quickly and was able to return to my nursing position after only two months. My sister's left kidney combined with the amazing team at Children's Hospital has given me the chance to return to graduate school to pursue my master's in nursing, a plan I always had that was solidified when another nurse, this time a nurse-practitioner, took wonderful care of me throughout the transplant care. I plan to finish this degree and spend my time taking care of those in my community. I have a few nurse-practitioner role models who have acted as both my nurses and my mentors. They care for and educate those around them, and I very much look up to them. I have one more health "blip" to move past, and then I hope to soon be as great a caregiver and a teacher as they are.

Maybe this is a good place to say that I may not have had the chance to tell this story without a new kidney. If you believe in helping others have a second chance like I've had, please, please sign up to become an organ donor today. An easy way to register is on your driver's license—and make certain you tell your family that this is your wish.

—ANNIE

Spending the majority of my first semester of middle school in the hospital guided my career interests from a goal of being an Olympic swimmer to a firm plan to be a nurse.

Preservation of a Legacy

I worry a lot about our country and its future for those who follow us, and I cannot help but think of all the reasons we felt such pride in belonging here. It has given us freedom, the chance to work hard with a sense of accomplishment, a sense of place, and the unified belief that we are here because it is a better place.

This is also what was instilled in me at a young age on my island.

There are seven generations of my family on Cumberland Island, Georgia, the largest barrier island on the East Coast. My great-great-grandfather came over from Scotland with his family and worked very hard for his success. From the time my family purchased Cumberland in the 1880s, a sense of respect and responsibility to the land was instilled in each generation.

There is a long overlay of human occupancy on Cumberland, from thousands of Timucua Indians, Spanish Revolutionary heroes, the Plantation era, homesteaders, and finally, my family. The island has been transformed many times with clear cutting for lumber for shipbuilding, cotton fields, and Spanish missions. What we see now is more than a hundred years of our family allowing the island to grow back and remain one of the most unspoiled islands on the East Coast.

There are guidelines the family set for building, so that no homes are ever built on the beach side, to ensure eighteen miles are unimpaired by anything. The roads remain dirt roads as they were before us.

As the branches of our family diffused and the worry of selling out became apparent, the entire family responded by creating the Cumberland Island National Seashore, assuring that there will never be any development or even a bridge to the island. Now, the public is allowed to come and experience the preservation of both cultural and natural resources through the integrity and responsibility of those who have lived here.

Every one of us who lives on Cumberland continues to do so with a great sense of responsibility to protect and preserve the legacy. Our home is now a small inn, run by family. Guests are offered the experience of elegant simplicity. There are no phones or TVs; instead, there are fresh garden vegetables, clamming, fishing, oystering, and naturalists who will educate you to the natural and cultural history of the island.

Those of us who live here work closely with the National Park Service and the state of Georgia to help fund non-game protection and protection of the historic buildings that remain on the island.

The island has provided so much to all of us in the family. It has instilled values and responsibility, and it doesn't matter whether any of us has been financially successful or struggling—Cumberland is always here for us. There is no sense of young or old; we are all a part of this and rejoice in our gatherings every year. Our elders taught us wisely that this is being handed to us momentarily to hold on to and protect for future generations, and we do so very seriously. I believe that true values come from a sense of belonging and a sense of responsibility to protect our surroundings, whether natural or cultural. Every day the island gives me the chance to continue to protect and preserve it, and with that, the opportunity to be true to myself.

—GOGO

Our elders taught us wisely that this island is being handed to us to momentarily hold on to and protect for future generations, and we do so very seriously.

Irresistible

My sister lives on the West Coast, and I live on the East, so we don't see each other as much as we'd like. She had told me that she'd found a lost Chihuahua a while back, and though she'd put up signs, went on Craigslist, and the whole nine yards, no one claimed the pup. So she adopted the little dog for good. As time went by, our dad had a stroke and came to live with her, and between that and other life issues, the dog just got to be too much for my sister to handle. When my husband, Randy, and I went out to visit, my sister told me that the dog had to go—it was the one thing she could figure out that would make her life a little easier.

My sister couldn't find anyone to take the dog, and feared the worst-case scenario would be Almond's fate. But once I saw the little Chihuahua, I fell in love. I wanted to take her, but Randy didn't. He was not pro-dog—we're both away from home a lot, and he was afraid she'd be lonely with our long days at work. So during the whole trip, Randy and I felt this unspoken friction between us. As we entered my sister's house to say good-bye, Randy stopped me and said, "Don't make me be the jerk." We left Almond behind, and I pouted all the way to the airport—until Randy turned the car around. It took the rest of the day to get the dog's papers and everything else in order, but we managed to make the red-eye flight that night. Now Almond lives happily with us across the country, although she's been renamed The Contessa, as it's clear she's taken over our house in an extremely regal way. She's the little dog who has had two second chances . . . so far!

—CINDY

Considering the Alternative

Many years ago, I had lost my job and was feeling terrible, desolate, every day at loose ends. In the back of my mind, I knew I really wanted to be a writer. But I felt broken and sad, useless in a way I didn't understand. I couldn't have sat down and written a paragraph, that's for sure. I would find reasons to leave the house, even if it was just grocery shopping or going to the dry cleaner's. But getting out in the world didn't help any; in fact, I would come home and say to my girlfriend that I felt like everyone on the street was looking at me, thinking, "Why is that guy out and about during the day, just hanging around? Doesn't he have a job?" And she said to me, "Maybe they think you're a writer, out getting some air and mulling over an idea, working out a plot point."

It was like magic. I know it sounds crazy, but those words changed everything for me. They helped clock my brain out of its misery, and suddenly, I felt optimistic. Of course, I was still undone by being let go from my job—that shakes a person's ego—but I felt confident suddenly, and yes, soon after that, I started writing, and I have built a successful career. And now, if I feel people on the street are looking at me, I have to assume it's because I have soup on my shirt.

—PETER

A Dream Realized

I was seventeen years old and in the final semester of my senior year of high school. I remember talking to my guidance counselor, whose words to me were, "Well, you're not planning on going on to college, right?" If my counselor believed I wasn't college material, it must be true. Convinced that I wasn't worthy of anything good, I quickly replied, "Oh, no, not at all." After I graduated from high school, I did make a feeble attempt at taking a few college-level classes, but I didn't stick with it. I tried again in my mid-twenties, but my performance was lukewarm at best. I still didn't believe I had the right to be in college.

Flash forward to the year 2000.... My second husband and beautiful seven-year-old daughter and I moved to a small town. Recently, I'd been having dreams of attending classes that were so vivid, I'd wake with a physical ache, wanting so badly to be in school. I'd never shared this feeling with a soul, thinking I was seriously too old for college. Then, this wonderful husband of mine, my dearest friend, asked me how I wanted to spend time at our new spot in the world. There was a community college nearby I could attend, or would I rather work instead? At that moment, my whole world changed. I pared down my priorities to God, family, and school. Recognizing this opportunity for the gift it was, I gave all I had and worked hard. My husband believed in me—that was really all I needed. Someone to believe in me. Somewhere in there, I learned to believe in me, too! I graduated summa cum laude and went on to earn my master's of science with an emphasis on speech and hearing sciences. A few years ago, I was hired for my dream position as a medical speech language pathologist. My strong and capable daughter is in college herself today, having had a college-student mom as a role model.

—KATHIE

I'd been having dreams. . . .
I'd wake with a physical ache,
wanting so badly to be in school.

A Fair Shot

A young man that I know of got into a little argument with his family at seventeen years old.

As a result, he ended up homeless.

Out there on the streets, he was hungry and chose to break into a restaurant.

The restaurant had no money and little food.

The young man ended up with a couple of tuna fish sandwiches, enough to curb his appetite.

But the young man wasn't a master thief and was quickly caught and charged with a felony.

He went to court without a lawyer, and the judge sent him to prison for one to two years despite having no prior record.

The judge stated that he was doing this because the accused was too young to be on his own.

After serving his sentence, the young man wanted to make his life whole.

He wanted to do something good.

He tried to join the marines. They rejected him because of his felony.

He tried to join the army. They rejected him because of his felony.

He tried to find a steady job. They rejected him because of his felony.

He floundered around for about five years, working menial jobs where he could get them.

Then he got a draft notice to the army, which no longer cared about his felony.

Given the opportunity to make right, the young man served honorably and, after being discharged, found employment and never made the same mistake again.

I'm proud to say that young man is me.

Ironically, it took the draft for society to give me, a felon, a chance.

But not every young man out there today is as lucky as me.

Today, I am a state senator, and I am fighting for a bill that is a set of hiring policies for private employers, designed to ensure that applicants with criminal records are evaluated on the merits of their qualifications, not on their criminal records.

We have too many hardworking people trying to find jobs who are being disqualified.

We need to give everyone who is looking for a job a fair shot.

I will continue to fight for an employment system that is fair to all our communities, so young people that made a mistake like me are not punished for the rest of their lives.

—ED

The Art Class

Little kids have no rights. A lot of times, they don't get to choose what it is they want to do—at least they didn't back in the day. Such was the case with me and my sister, Danielle. Like lots of mothers, ours signed us up for lessons when we were young: Danielle was going to go take art classes, and I would take ballet. I hated it from the start. So did Danielle. The truth was *she* wanted to go to dancing school and *I* wanted to take the art classes. But it was not to be. So we got dragged to our appointed lessons, hating every minute. It probably goes without saying that, fifty years later, I don't dance, and she doesn't draw.

Time passed, as it does, and I grew up and got a good job—feminism opened the floodgates, and I became a chiropractor. Now the wannabe artist had a "Dr." in front of her name. Don't get me wrong; I loved my work. I was lucky enough to form a practice with my best friend—it thrived for many, many years, and we made wonderful friends and a good living. But after almost three decades of doing this physically punishing work, my partner's body rebelled, and mine followed a few years later. It was enough. I have now joined a friend in his newest venture, and have my fingers in several of his pies, including restaurant and culinary ventures, which bring me back to my teenage days working with my father, who was a renowned Washington, DC, restaurateur.

But more importantly, about ten years ago, I started to paint. I have a little one-car garage that I turned into a studio, and on weekends, I retreat there and just let loose. I adored it from the very start: It felt like home, and so I kept at it, and yes, I finally took classes. It seemed like I had some talent, but I needed to begin to learn all the things I never had the chance to tap into all those years ago. And then my work started to sell. People bought it. At first, just a little, but now, I'm actually making a living selling my paintings. Is it a doctor's salary? No. Is it an incredible dream fulfilled? Yes. And it's because I never forgot what I wanted. It may have taken a long time for me to get back there, but I knew that I would.

—MICHELE

The Principal's Award

After a certain point in my freshman year, my principal, Sister A., called me in and said, "Let's save some paper, Mary Seton. Assume you have detention unless you hear otherwise." I even spent Saturdays folding napkins in the basement of the convent.

Recently, Sister A. came to see me in a dream when I was ill, appearing like a beacon—or maybe a nightmare. What was she doing there? There couldn't possibly be more detention. I had served my time. "It's not all fun is it, Mary Seton?" she said. "Not everything is a joke, people are depending on you to make decisions. They need you." I assumed she was speaking about my business and the folks who worked for me. But why was she back to bother me? I had been, after all, her Achilles heel. Everyone knew that. I was always out of uniform. I stole the teachers' bathroom key over and over again and placed it right inside my locker with a sign that said "Teachers' Bathroom Key Here." She knew. I knew she knew. She never stooped down to my level though. Sister A. didn't stoop to anyone's level. Teachers, parents, the Holy Father, the students, we were all afraid of her. She never raised her voice. She never threw things. She was just herself.

One week, word came down that Sister A.'s father had died. We had never thought of her as a person with a family;

we thought she had arrived on earth fully formed as Sister A. I didn't like the idea of funerals, and I knew this would be a mandatory all-school mass. I just did not want to go, and I felt strongly about it. I girded myself and said to her, "Sister, I'm sorry about your loss, but I don't like funerals, and I don't believe in God. I cannot attend your father's funeral mass." I waited for the wrath. As usual, she had no expression. And then she touched my shoulder, looked me in the eye, and said, "You are excused from mass today, Mary Seton. I'm sure you'll find something useful to do in the library. You will be unsupervised." I realized I had a chance to show her what I was really made of. She knew in that moment that there was more to me, and in that moment, I knew it, too.

I graduated at the bottom of my class, but at the ceremony, I received the principal's award—the highest honor in the school—anyway. Sister A. and I shook hands solemnly as my classmates and the teachers cheered. "Mary won!" they screamed. I had brought down the wicked witch! But had I really? In that one moment, she had changed my life. She had made me understand that to lead, you had to love. You had to be bigger than anything around you. You had to find the way in the dark. You had to care. Leading was not edicts, it was in caring about the people you led, always introducing the intangibles of life into the equation, always wanting to do the right thing.

I didn't go out to change the world that graduation day. It would take many decades before I introduced the word "we" into my vocabulary. But when I did, it came out naturally. I knew who I was, and I was ready to do what I knew I could do, what I was meant to do: to lead.

—MARY SETON ON SISTER A.

NOTE: Mary Seton passed away shortly before this book's publication. Sister A. was right—"they" did need her. Mary left behind one of the country's very first urban farms, which lives on as a highly successful nonprofit community venture.

I realized I had a chance to show her what I was really made of. She knew in that moment that there was more to me, and in that moment I knew it, too.

The Hurricane

It took Mother Nature for me to find my community.

Late in the season in 2012, Hurricane Sandy rocked the East Coast, causing untold damage from the Caribbean up to New England. My family lives in Rockaway Beach, Queens, one of the hardest hit locations of Sandy's wrath. And I have to begin by saying we were not as watchful as we might have been. The year before, our shore community completely evacuated when we were warned of Hurricane Irene, and then we were not affected by the storm. So the next year, it seemed people were not so quick to pick up and leave home when we heard that Sandy was coming up the coast.

I live on the beach in a co-op apartment with a lovely ocean view; my parents live three blocks away. When I offered to come stay with them as the alerts of Sandy became more serious, they waved me off. But when Sandy came—well, I thought I was going to die in either water or fire that night. I could see fire over near where my parents lived. The boardwalk was totally lifted up, gone. Cars like little toys, floating down the street. No lights, no phones, nothing, nothing, nothing.

My friend climbed out the fire escape in our building to go check on my parents while it was still dark out the next morning; I'm on the fourth floor, and we couldn't go down to the lobby because there was eight feet of water. When the water went back out, there was four feet of sand—the super finally had to dig a path for us to get out the back. When my friend came back and told me Mom and Dad were all right, I was undone. He helped me pack a bag and get over to their house. When I finally got outside and saw what everything was like, I just cried and cried. No one had any food, nothing, no one had prepared for this.

My family was OK, which was the most important thing. My neighborhood is filled with firemen and policemen, and that's what you want at a time like this, people who know what to do in an emergency. Everyone brought whatever food they had out into the street to share. Meanwhile, my parents' basement was destroyed, and they ran upstairs without a morsel of food or drink. You know the Italians: No matter how beautiful the house is, they have to live in the basement so everything can stay nice upstairs!

People outside the community came in droves—I've never seen this kind of volunteering. Blankets, water, food— for weeks and weeks people came. I'm in construction, so we called an electrician friend of ours, and he came a few days later. The neighbors started coming over, asking for his help. He stayed and took care of everyone. Neighbors thanked my family, saying, "Because of you, my children have light and water. Thank you." So many people came to help, with no agenda.

But our own community came together in a way I never saw before. It didn't matter if you were Italian or Irish or

Jewish; it mattered that you were a neighbor of mine, and you survived. I respect the neighborhood and the people in it way more than I ever did before. Businesses? I do most of my shopping there now. I switched my prescriptions. I go to the butcher. Before, I was always, "No, I'm a city girl, everything for me is there." Not anymore. There isn't a thing I wouldn't do for my community now. I walk into the grocery store, and it's, "How's your mom and dad, the loveliest people ever?"

My parents had a trunk they came here from Italy with. It was in the basement, and after we were allowed back into our homes more than two months later—we had all moved to my brother's home in another county while our area began it's long cleanup journey—I went over to my parents', and my father was out in the yard. He was carefully taking the few things that were still in one piece out of the trunk. He first kissed every single thing, every photograph—maybe thirty out of a huge trunk—and then he patted them and carefully put them in the sun to dry. Look, we still have what we came to this country with.

It changed me forever. I look out my window at the ocean now and I think, "I respect you way more than I ever did before. Because you are way more powerful than any of us could ever imagine."

But we rebuild. That's what we do.

—STELLA ANNA

But also our own community came together in a way I never saw before. It didn't matter if you were Italian or Irish or Jewish; it mattered that you were a neighbor of mine, and you survived.

Acknowledgments

As always, the first people I want to thank, so very deeply, are my friends at Abrams Books, who, time after time, have given me the go-ahead when I've said, "Really, this is a great idea!" They believe in me and do right by me every time. At the top of this list is always Michael Jacobs, who gave me a very big second chance himself. David Cashion and Mary Wowk are always there backing me up, and their faith in me gives me faith in myself. The rest of the Abrams team makes me feel like family, every day.

Of course the contributors who told their stories here are the heroes and heroines of this book, and I can't thank them enough. Many were eager to share their experiences, happy to recall the results and share their positive outcome with others. "Here, see, it can be done," they seem to say. Others had a hard time going back, but I do believe every single person featured in this volume felt elation, gratitude, conviction, joy—some positive feeling when he or she got the story on the page.

I especially want to thank Aiisha Snipes-England, who tells her very difficult story here. Hearing her experience, and how it affected her, affected *me* so much that it became the turning point of constructing this book. I realized that everyone opening his or her heart here needed a personal and particular understanding of his or her life and emotions, and I began to find that working together, having conversations, writing drafts together—all this often helped pry open some rusty doors and memories. Aiisha opened her heart so wide and with such dignity that it somehow made me understand how difficult a healing process can be—and how unknowing we are of people's vast interiors.

And mostly a thank-you to my dad; even now, many years after he's been gone, those who loved him laugh at what a relentless optimist he was. I am very, very lucky that he passed that trait on to me, and I treasure it. For me, there's always another chance, another bit of excitement, just around the bend.

About the Author

Erin McHugh is a former publishing executive and the award-winning author of more than twenty-five books of trivia, history, children's titles, and more, including *One Good Deed: 365 Days of Trying to Be Just a Little Bit Better*. She lives in New York City.

Follow Erin on Twitter: @erinhere